Highlights

OF NORWAY

GRO STANGELAND   EVA VALEBROKK

OF NORWAY

Translated and edited by Alison Arderne Olsen

WENNERGREN-CAPPELEN A/S

Contents

PREFACE

Not even the glossy pictures in the tourist brochures can convey the breathtaking beauty of the Norwegian landscape. It has to be experienced to be properly appreciated. And for hundreds of years visitors have been coming to Norway to admire the fantastic scenery, the mountains, forests, and fjords.

And yet the country has so much more to offer than beautiful scenery and the midnight sun. We wanted to present a broader view, to take the visitor into lesser-known corners of the country as well as throwing new light on some of the more celebrated attractions. It was not our intention to make this purely a picture-book, even though the illustrations have been chosen with care. We wanted to show glimpses of artistic and cultural life, of traditions and history, of a way of thinking and a way of being. We introduce the reader to Norwegian poets, writers, and artists, some of them well known, others less familiar, all of whom were, or are, of great influence in their time.

We have chosen a selection of sights and monuments, towns and museums, walks and journeys, the length and breadth of Norway. The descriptions are not intended to be exhaustive, but to provide an indication of the pleasures in store for the visitor.

This is a book for connoisseurs of Norway – it shows Norway from the inside, through Norwegian eyes. We hope it will illuminate something of the character and history of the Norwegian people, which have been shaped by their mountains, their long seaboard, and their isolated inland valleys.

We wish you a pleasant and interesting journey.

RØROS

If you have ever visited the mining towns of Harz, in Germany, you will experience a strong feeling of recognition as you walk down the street called Bergmannsgata in Røros. Surely, you will say, this cannot be a coincidence?

Nor is it. The mining town of Røros was the result of a meeting in 1644 between a farmer and a German mining engineer. The farmer was out hunting reindeer in the Storvola area, and in their flight the animals kicked away some earth and exposed a stone with an attractive shine. Hans Aasen took the stone home and showed it to Lorentz Lossius, who worked at the nearby Kvikne mine and who sometimes called in on Aasen on his way to exploit a claim he had staked in the neighbourhood. Lossius realized at once that this was copper, and mining operations were immediately started in the area, whose name was changed to Storwarts. This was the main mine of the Røros Mining Company, Røros Bergverk, for almost 300 years.

Christian IV of Denmark and Norway was of an extravagant nature, and spent money on a grand scale. He did not endear himself to the Norwegian people, but he had great plans for Norway, and was responsible for founding a

number of towns, among them Kristiania, Kristiansand, Kongsberg, and of course Røros. The copper mines received royal privileges as early as 1646, only two years after the rich vein of copper had been discovered. The privileges entitled the company to exploit woodland, ore, and watercourses within a 40-kilometre radius of

the Storwarts mine. Furthermore, the farmers who lived inside this radius were under an obligation to work in the mines. On the other hand, "schools for reading and arithmetic" were also established at an early date; the director of the mines had no wish to employ illiterate and "ignorant creatures".

Røros grew up around the first smelting works, which was built in 1646, and the miners' church, which was completed in 1650. When the Swedes burnt down Røros in 1678 only the church was saved, after first being used as a stable. However, the church soon became too small and was considered too "simple", so in 1784 the present one was built, an octagonal baroque building with the characteristic miner's sign on the tower, and seating for 2000 people, a large church by the standards of the time. There was even a royal pew, curtained for privacy, and enclosed pews for the high society of the town. A unique feature of the church is the position of the altarpiece, organ, and pulpit, one above the other on the same wall. The stone for the church was taken from the local quarry, and the mining company lent their best craftsmen to oversee the building work. One of Norway's greatest novelists, Johan Falkberget, is buried in the cemetery here.

Low German was frequently to be heard in the streets of Røros – like so many other Norwegian mining companies, the Røros company turned to Germany in search of expertise. The number of mines expanded, and by the eighteenth century the copper mines at Røros were among the largest in Europe, and represented a major Norwegian industrial concern, employing 4000 men. However, the activities of the mine were very hard on the surrounding countryside, especially the woodland. Gunpowder had not yet been invented, and wood and charcoal were used in large quantities, especially in the smelting works. During the calcination of the ore, too, quantities of suphur dioxide were released, which poisoned the surrounding vegetation. As a result of this, Røros now lies on a windswept heath, with little vegetation, surrounded by the

slag heaps characteristic of mining activity.

The mine prospered until about 1814, when it entered a gradual period of decline until the First World War, which improved its fortunes. After this it again declined, and by 1931 it was only saved by the finding of a new vein of ore. In 1977, however, the mine was closed for the last time; at this point it was Norway's oldest functioning industrial concern.

Now mining has been replaced by tourism as the town's major source of revenue. The mining village of Røros was made a pilot project for the Architectural Heritage Year in 1975, and is now on UNESCO's World Heritage List. It remains an attractive example of an inland mining town, with its main street of fine houses belonging to directors of the mine and higher civil servants, its unique church, and the small miners' houses along Slaggveien. Røros has inspired many ar-

tists, the most notable being Harald Sohlberg [1869–1935], whose neo-romantic paintings of the church and streets of Røros have done much to draw attention to the beauty and charm of the town. Another well-known name associated with Røros is that of Johan Falkberget [1879–1967], a novelist who started out as a miner. His novels set in Røros, of which perhaps the most famous is *The Fourth Night Watch*, have been translated into several languages.

In the museum the reconstructed smelting works contains models of the mining machinery, and there are guided tours around the mine Olavsgruva, which lies about 13 kilometres from the town centre. Inside Olavsgruva is Norway's most original theatre and concert hall, called Bergmannshallen.

FOKSTUMYRA

It has been said of Fokstumyra that "One should spend a whole night on the marsh, listening to all the voices joining in unison to form a haunting choir that gives an almost supernatural feeling." In order to really appreciate this sanctuary, one should visit it at night or "in the evening, when the last rays of daylight shine rose-red above the mighty dome of Snøhetta [the highest mountain peak in the Dovre chain]."

Fokstumyra is situated high up in the Dovre mountain chain, one of the most magnificent in a country that specializes in mountains. The marsh lies 950 metres above sea level and is about 7.5 square kilometres in extent. Mountain birch and juniper, osier, moss and grasses cover the ground, and the area is a paradise for birds, especially waders. Here we can find different varieties of duck, crane, the black-throated diver, redshank, wood sandpiper, snipe, lapwing, curlew, and the golden plover with its melancholy cry. Rich as it is in insect life, the marsh also provides food for many smaller birds, like thrushes and bluethroats. Among the 130 species of birds that have been registered there are also game birds: ptarmigan and grouse, and birds of prey, like the hen harrier and merlin. Seventy species are registered as nesting there, and the area also acts as a resting and refreshment station for migrating birds.

For over 150 years Fokstumyra has been a mecca for birdwatchers. By the end of the eighteenth century there were many enthusiastic descriptions of the bird life and the beauty of the countryside. In his book *The Norwegian Countryside*, published in 1847, the forester J.S. Barth sang the praises of the marshland, which he assured the reader "would never need to fear that the busy farmer would channel its water or the all-devouring plough transform its appearance, nor that the noise of some bustling steam engine would disturb its peace and drive away the living creatures in its care."

Unfortunately Barth under-estimated the Norwegian Railways, and in 1916 the railway line was firmly laid right through the marsh from north to south, in spite of strong protests from birdlovers. But birds have a great capacity for adaptation, and soon the hen harrier and the short-eared owl were nesting within a few metres of the railway. Certain others, like the ruff

and great snipe, were frightened away, but since then have returned to nest.

The railway was not the greatest threat to the flora and fauna of the marsh, however. Fokstumyra became such a popular resort among collectors, both at home and abroad, that at one time there was a very real danger that it would be stripped of many of its plants, birds and eggs. It was therefore declared a national park in 1923, the first time such a status was granted to an area of Norway. Today there are strict rules regulating traffic in the area, especially between 25 April and 15 July, when no traffic is permitted anywhere except along marked paths. In addition, all animals and birds are protected all the year round. Egg collecting is naturally also for-

bidden, and nests and all kinds of animal lairs must be left undisturbed.

In addition to its animal life, the rich soil of the marsh provides excellent growth conditions for a variety of plants, some of them rare. And the marsh has interesting geological formations, in the form of drumlins, long ridges formed by glacial drift that show the direction of movement of the glaciers through the ages.

HEIDAL

"I smell the blood of a Christian man!"
snarled the trolls to the small boys who had to
cross Bjølstad wood from Vågå to Heidal in order to beg for food. But the little boys managed
to trick the three trolls into giving them the one
eye they shared, and in return they received silver and gold. And since that time no trolls have
been seen in Heidal Wood, according to the fairytale. But the atmosphere of trolls and fairytales

still clings to the hamlet of Heidal, which is one
of Norway's largest living museums.

The people of the valley of Gudbrandsdal
have taken good care of their beautiful and
characteristic old houses, but Heidal is particularly fine even by Gudbrandsdal standards. Of
the 400 buildings listed for conservation in the
whole of this long valley, 90 are to be found in
Heidal. There are 17 farms with at least one listed building, and nine which consist only of listed buildings. The oldest of these date back to
the sixteenth century. Heidal has also kept up
the old *seter* tradition, whereby the cows were
driven into the mountains for the summer, and a
cowherd, traditionally a beautiful young girl,

stad farm since the early 1600s, but it has not been in use since 1752, when another, larger church was built for the hamlet as a whole. In about 1820 it was pulled down and reassembled lower down the valley, where it served as a barn and storehouse. Today Bjølstad church has been restored and reassembled again next door to Heidal church. The oldest building at Bjølstad farm dates back to 1610, and there are a number of buildings from the eighteenth century as well. The magnificent Nystova building is from 1818. The farm has been in the hands of the Bratt family for 25 generations, ever since 1270.

Kruke is another fine example of a traditional farm, with its impressive collection of 20 listed farm buildings. Two well-known weavers, Ragnhild and Karen Prestegard, were brought up here and used to run a weaving school at the farm. Øvre Aaseng farm is best known for its main farmhouse from 1764, which contains much valuable furniture and other articles, and for the other eight listed buildings that form the main barton, or farmyard. This farm is also known for its crafts, particularly the Aaseng recorder, which has been made here for five generations. Another farm worth mentioning is Søre Harildstad, with its bell tower, its handsome carved pillars and its external galleries, which inspired many of the fairytale illustrations by Erik Werenskiold and Alf Rolfsen.

Many of these farms show groups of visitors around and provide refreshment if given prior notice, and some farms provide rented accommodation.

For those more actively inclined, Heidal can provide more than ancient culture. The river that runs through Gudbrandsdalen, the Sjoa River, which has only just escaped hydroelectric development and is now permanently protected, is regarded as one of the best rivers in the world for rafting and paddling. Since the popular new sport of rafting made its way over from America to Heidal, regular guided tours are arranged for rafters.

looked after them, milking them and making butter and cheese in a cabin high up in the mountains, all summer long. A whole folklore has grown up around these summer farms, in which the girl is often wooed by the young men of the village, and it is a favourite literary theme.

These listed farms are not museums. They cling to the valley sides, their ancient timber walls, burned almost silver by the sun, gleaming palely above the river. Bjølstad farm is the oldest, and in its heyday it was the largest farm in the whole valley, consisting of 700 buildings, including all the *seter* cabins and the 25 crofters' farms, and had its own church. The tiny log-built church has probably occupied its place on Bjøl-

THE NORWEGIAN FORESTRY MUSEUM

Although half the area of Norway lies above the timber line, only about 3 per cent of the remainder is cultivated, and large areas of the country are covered in forest. It is therefore not surprising that the country should have a unique Forestry Museum with a high international reputation. In 1980 it was given the European Museum of the Year Award by the Council of Europe.

Trapping, hunting and fishing are among man's oldest occupations. Agriculture had a late start in Norway, for geographical and climatic reasons, and for a long time it had to be supplemented by hunting and fishing in the forests and lakes. Apart from this, the forest had little commercial value until about 400 years ago, when timber became one of Norway's most important exports and in certain periods the backbone of her economy.

The Forestry Museum at Elverum shows how people have made use of the resources of woods and forests throughout history. Not only timber, game, and fish, but also berries, plants of all kinds, flowers, and trees, moss, lichen, and fungi, have all been exploited by man for various purposes. The Museum specializes in learning activities for the whole family, demonstrating the smelting of bog iron, the making of tar, and other age-old techniques, and in August holding hunting and fishing days, which are especially popular.

The floating of logs down the Norwegian rivers has always been the most efficient, but also the most dangerous and exciting method of transporting timber to the factories on the coast, whence they could be easily exported or transported to other parts of Norway in their finished form. About an hour's drive from Elverum, the Forestry Museum has established a subsidiary department for timber floating, at Sørlistøa, on the edge of the Osensjøen lake. The tugboat *Trysil-Knut*, which until recently hauled logs on Osensjøen, now takes tourists for trips around the lake, and on special fishing days visitors may try their hand at catching powan, or freshwater herring, and vendace.

Prestøya is an island in the Glomma river with an open-air museum combined with a recreational area. Here about 40 houses together with a sawmill, an exhibition of traps and trappers' equipment, and other local activities are displayed. In the middle of the island is an ideal picnic spot, and the woods are full of paths for ramblers. There is also a playground for children, where they can play freely and safely while the grown-ups drink their coffee in peace.

One of the primary purposes of the Forestry Museum is nonetheless to carry out research and conservation, as well as collecting and preserving. In addition to the departments of forestry, hunting, and trapping, there is a separate department for hunting weapons, where a selection of hunting implements showing their development from bows and arrows to modern rifles is displayed. The knife has played a prominent part in Norwegian cultural history, and as well as an exhibition of knives, demonstrations are held of how knives are made, a craft that is still very much alive in Norway. A smart new building contains exhibitions of workshops for boat-building and for making furniture, fiddles, knives and fishing implements. The production of tar, charcoal, and paper is shown, together with models of sawmills and sluice gates. The restaurant specializes in delicacies from the Norwegian forests, like salmon, freshwater herring, elk, roe deer and reindeer, cranberries and cloudberries – Norwegian cuisine at its best and most traditional.

In 1979 a mainly freshwater aquarium was opened, showing the various water habitats from the mountains to the sea. There is also a separate fish farming section where the visitor can follow the growth of the fish from fry to adulthood.

MAIHAUGEN

It is difficult to believe that the open-air museum of Maihaugen, with its 130 or so buildings spread over 25 acres of ground, and its extensive collections of objects and implements derived from the traditional Norwegian peasant culture, is due to the efforts of one man. Anders Sandvig was born in 1862 and after training as a dentist, he moved to Lillehammer in 1885 for reasons of health. Here he encountered the rich cultural tradition of the valley of Gudbrandsdalen, which inspired him with strong nationalistic feelings. This was in the spirit of the time; Norway had already achieved an independent constitution and was in the process of becoming a completely independent country. Sandvig rapidly became in-

terested in collecting objects that were distinctively Norwegian, and it is said that the first object he ever collected was a carved wooden beer mug dated 1678, the same mug he is depicted as holding in the statue that stands in the main square of Lillehammer. He himself relates that it was an altarpiece from the demolished Church of the Cross in Lillehammer that he first fell in love with. "I had the feeling one has when one suddenly meets a person one feels terribly sorry for, and wishes in vain one could stretch out a helping hand", he wrote in his memoirs. Finally he did manage to stretch out a helping hand, even though he had to pay for it in installments, and the altarpiece can now be seen in Garmo Stave Church in Maihaugen.

Now seriously gripped by collector's fever, Sandvig continued to dismay the good burghers of Lillehammer by buying up "worthless rubbish". In 1887, for example, he was on his way to a dentists' congress in Copenhagen when

he came across a seventeenth-century cupboard, also from a church. He promptly spent the money for the journey on the cupboard and had to return home to Lillehammer. He began a series of twice-yearly journeys the length of Gudbrandsdalen, which were advertised in advance by posters. The farmers were more sympathetic to his motives than the citizens of Lillehammer, and everywhere he went people gathered with their toothache and, more important, with objects and articles of furniture for sale.

After some time he also began to collect the actual farm buildings. Norwegian farms consist of a collection of small, specialized buildings grouped round a yard, or barton, and constructed of notched logs. This makes them relatively easy to transport, and Sandvig began collecting these and reassembling them in his garden. For example, the farm of Bjørnstad, which can be seen at Maihaugen today, consists of 26 separate buildings, which were used for storage, cooking, baking, brewing, housing the animals, summer accommodation, and winter accommodation. One of Sandvig's aims was to share his knowledge with others, and he soon opened the collection to the public. His visitors' book is full of the names of well-known contemporaries, as well as a surprising number of foreigners.

Sandvig distinguished himself from the majority of contemporary collectors, however, by his discrimination. He consciously based his collection on regional principles, and chose the buildings according to strict criteria, and he was very careful to match the interiors to the buildings, rather than using the rooms merely as display cabinets. His views on cultural history were strongly influenced by the national and social revolutions that were taking place all over Europe, and by the ideas of Charles Darwin and the Norwegian sociologist Eilert Sundt, who had published a number of works on social conditions in Norway.

In 1901 he sold his collection to the Lillehammer Association, and Maihaugen gradually came into being, a regional, open-air museum whose aim was to preserve Norwegian cultural history in a systematic way. This was unusual at a time when most people were trying to forget Norway's past, which was strongly associated with Danish and Swedish cultural dominance. Thus Maihaugen showed the daily life and activities of the people of Gudbrandsdalen through the ages. This was made especially effective by Sandvig's ability to position buildings in such a way that they appeared to have been there for ever.

Today Maihaugen comprises more than Gudbrandsdalen. It has buildings and displays from all over Norway, among them a collection of about 30 workshops from different parts of the country showing traditional crafts and trades, and a reconstructed town, which is used among other things to house various public offices. There is also the large hall, Store Maihaugsal, with the magnificent backdrop formed by Jacob Weideman's brilliantly colourful painting *Mai*. The beauties of

the surrounding parkland are much appreciated by visitors, and on Midsummer's Eve the whole museum is taken over by the inhabitants of Lillehammer themselves, who flock to Maihaugen to experience the traditional festivities celebrated in traditional dress.

KONGSVINGER CASTLE

"If we can only beat the Swedes, we don't care about the rest of the world!" The rivalry between Sweden and Norway goes back a long way. It now takes a relatively peaceful form, mainly confined to the Olympics and other sporting events, but 300 years ago the Norwegians meant it literally, and a chain of forts was built along the Swedish border to keep the arch-enemy in their place.

In those days the main route from Norway to Sweden ran through Kongsvinger. It was not a good road; the English traveller Edward Clarke complained bitterly that it took a whole day to travel three and a half Danish miles [about 26 kilometres], and that this, added to the fact that the inns were terrible, made him and his companions regret that they had not waited until the winter, when frost and snow made the roads easier to travel. In spite of this, it was a much travelled highway, so that it was natural that the first bulwark against marauding Swedes should be erected at the ferry landing stage on the Glomma River. The position was excellent, and under Christian V the local *stattholder* Ulrik Frederik Gyldenløwe started to build the fortress that eventually became Kongsvinger Castle in 1673. From 1675 to 1679 a war raged along the frontier, and as a result a number of fortresses were built or reinforced all along the Swedish border. In 1682 a permanent garrison was established at Kongsvinger Castle under the command of Lieutenant-Colonel Georg Reichwein.

The castle's strategic position, however, proved in itself to be such a strong deterrent that its guns have never fired a shot in anger. It has never been surrounded or attacked, even during border conflicts when there were Swedish troops in the area. In 1808, for example, the Swedish vanguard reached as far as the Glomma River, but there they remained, daunted by the guns of Kongsvinger. And in 1814, during the Napoleonic Wars, the Swedes were defeated at the border itself, and never managed to get as far as the castle.

The castle reached its heyday during the years around 1808, when the permanent garrison numbered 900 men. During the whole period from 1741 to 1823 slaves were employed here, and one of the buildings is still known as "The Slave Quarters". The living conditions of slaves and soldiers had always been very bad, in fact they were known to be the worst of any Norwegian castle, and although some attempts were made to improve their lot, even in 1808 the mortality was high.

After the end of the Napoleonic Wars and the establishment of an independent constitution for Norway in 1814, the importance of

Kongsvinger Castle began to decline, and in 1823 it was decided to remove the cannon. A military garrison was retained, however, and at the end of the century, when relations with the Swedes again became critical owing to the Norwegian desire for complete independence, the castle was strengthened by the addition of two forts in the neighbourhood and increasing numbers of artillerymen. Up to 30 men were to be employed, and set to work at various tasks; they were to be paid 2.50 crowns a day and had to supply their own food and clothing. The numbers were further increased during the summer until the garrison had up to 1000 men. Again, however, a peaceful solution was arrived at, and the union between Sweden and Norway was dissolved without a shot being fired.

Since that time military activity at Kongsvinger has been peaceful, with the exception of a couple of skirmishes in 1940. During the occupation the castle was taken over by German troops, and Norwegian prisoners were put to work there. Quisling himself donated a gymnastics hall. After the liberation the situation was reversed, and the castle was used as an internment camp for Norwegian collaborators. Today it is occupied by the Home Guard and by a museum.

THE ANCIENT HIGHWAYS

First, there were the waterways – the sea, the rivers, and the lakes. On land there were goat, sheep, and cattle tracks. When the first traces of man and horses began to make their mark on the Norwegian landscape, carriages and chariots had long been thundering along broad, stone-paved highways in the countries further south.

The remains of these ancient highways can be found in several places in Norway, especially on both sides of the Oslo fjord, in the counties of Vestfold and Østfold. Here they show up as deep or shallow U-shaped depressions, clearly visible in the landscape. The ancient highway of Hunn in Østfold is a classical example of such a prehistoric way. Road no. 110, for example, from Fredrikstad to Skjeberg, runs parallel to the old highway, and takes the traveller past the sites of ancient settlements called Begby, Broge, Hunn, Gunnarstorp, Hornes, and Solberg, which are unusually rich in sights and monuments of archaeological and historical interest.

Among these cultural monuments are rock carvings depicting ships and four-wheeled chariots, suns, processions, dancers and fighters. The reasons for these carvings will always remain a mystery: what were the artists trying to express?

The fields of carvings at Begby, Hornes and Solberg are large and richly stocked with petroglyphs, and are thought to have originated from the Late Bronze Age, about 1000–500 BC. They were made by an agricultural society and have a religious content, with symbols indicating

sun worship and a fertility cult. The Solberg field, for example, has a figure with a sun wheel and a sword. The name Solberg [the Norwegian word *sol* means "sun"] is thought to indicate that rites of sun worship were practised here. The large variety of motifs, which differ considerably from the motifs of the hunting cultures that also made rock carvings in this part of the world, provide interesting indications of the way the people of the time lived, the implements they used, and the kind of ships they built. Thus, although the symbolic value of the carvings is difficult to interpret, their historical value is immense.

These carvings, like almost everywhere else where such Bronze Age carvings are found, are

in an area of fertile farmland, which tells us something about the cultural landscape here as well, and how long it has been farmed. Other Bronze Age activities were trade and shipping, and it is not surprising that ships play such a large part in the carvings. The Hunn field lies at the crossroads of two highways, one leading inland and one leading to the innermost tip of Tostekilen inlet. These fields are all fairly close to the sea and contain some of the largest collections of ship petroglyphs in the country. At Hornes, for example, there is a rock with over 20 ships on it, all sailing in the same direction. At Skærviken, where there used to be a good harbour in the nearby inlet, there are signs that horse-racing was held in prehistoric times.

The fields of rock carvings along this particular highway are thought to have been places of worship, where the carvings were made in connection with religious ceremonies. The old farms also lay along the highway, and there were many old graves in this area. The graves found at the Hunn field, which was excavated in 1950–52, were mostly fire graves, but there are also two graves from the time of the Romans and the Viking era respectively. The former, which was a very rich find, probably belonged to a chief. Burial mounds have been found at Gunnarstorp, as well as groups of stones and individual menhirs, and there are indications that there are more graves in existence below the ground here.

THE OLD TOWN, FREDRIKSTAD

A walk along the ramparts, for purposes of courting, playing, walking the dog, or just admiring the view is a time-hallowed Fredrikstad custom, which has been going on for so long that a local dialect word has even been coined for it.

The Old Town in Fredrikstad is the only surviving fortified town in Scandinavia. It was founded in 1567 by Frederik II of Denmark-Norway, and was the first Norwegian town to be called after a king. Like so many towns of the period, it was ravaged by fire, not once but several times, and now only the ramparts remain from the first century of the town's history.

Less than a century after the town had been founded, relations became strained between Frederik III of Denmark-Norway and Carl X Gustaf of Sweden, and in 1658 the Swedes captured the fortress of Bohus and took the whole

Swedes. In 1663 Frederik III approved the plans drawn up by Quartermaster General William Coucheron for a fortress with five bastions, a moat, and a drawbridge.

In 1665 the new king, Christian V, inspected the completed fortress, which had been equipped with 130 cannon, and expressed himself well pleased. Indeed, it was the largest and best equipped fortress in Norway, especially as regards artillery. The townspeople, however, were not as happy as the king; on the contrary, their lives were completely overturned by the new developments. Among other things they were obliged to provide lodgings for up to 2000 soldiers in wartime. And if there had been fires before, there were twice as many now. Hundreds of houses, mostly built of wood, were crammed into the narrow spaces between the ramparts, and created a veritable fire trap. It is said of the history of Fredrikstad that it consists of three volumes, two volumes of fires and one of crises. Military considerations came into continuous conflict with civil ones, especially commercial activities. The greatest problem, however, was that the commanders of the fortress, who usually had high military rank, failed to respect the position of the civil authorities, and often overruled the mayor and town council. Nothing could have been less representative of the inscription above the main gate, which proclaimed "iustitia" and "pietate", justice and mercy, alongside King Christian V's monogram. Conditions became so bad that the citizens sent letters of complaint to the king: "We who, struck down by poverty and ruined by fire, are forced to creep into the miserable few remaining houses, are further obliged to bear the unutterable burden of the billeting [of large numbers of soldiers]". And in 1713 the parish priest, the notary public, and the mayor all signed a prayer addressed to the king, which concluded as follows: "God help us bear the

of the province of Bohuslän from Norway. This meant that Fredrikstad, together with Halden, now marked the south-eastern border against Sweden, and it became imperative to erect fortifications to prevent further incursions by the

commander imposed on us ... but above all we beg and pray in all humility that we may be delivered from him or him from us."

Nor could the sight of the slave quarters, or the market place with its gallows and pillory, have improved matters. The slave quarters, which housed prisoners, were in use right up to 1848, when they were all transferred to Akershus Castle in Oslo.

Although the town had certain privileges, such as the sole right to all trade within a radius of thirty kilometres, and the right to grant asylum to bankrupts and dissenters, a seldom-used privilege, the situation became so bad that the townspeople began moving to the west side of the river. Finally the authorities could no longer ignore the situation, and legitimized it by formally declaring the west side of the river a suburb of the town and subject to its jurisdiction.

During the 1850s sawmills were no longer subject to licensing requirements, and a number of mills were set up on the west bank of the river. Soon timber and other trades began to flourish in this part of town, which became the centre of commercial activity, and by the beginning of this century the old town was in a steady decline. In 1903 the fortress was closed down as a military base, but since there was so little activity in the neighbourhood, it was not thought necessary to pull down the buildings. And this is why we are able to enjoy the well-preserved old town today, and to walk of an evening along the ramparts. And what we see is not so very different from the sight that greeted Christian V as he proceeded on his round of inspection. The king would almost certainly have felt at home there today, and, like the gentle, amiable man he was, he would have enjoyed the sight of well-fed, contented soldiery [there is still a military garrison here] and the idyllic atmosphere, which has made the town such an attractive place to visit.

FREDRIKSTEN CASTLE

Unlike so many Norwegian fortified castles, Fredriksten Castle in Halden, or Fredrikshald, as the town was known until 1928, has seen a good deal of fighting, and has experienced some of the most dramatic incidents in Norwegian military history. Thus, Charles XII of Sweden was put to flight after his first attack on Fredriksten in 1716. In order to prevent the Swedes from gaining the castle, the town was set on fire by its own inhabitants, and after the battle the castle walls rose proudly above the smoking ruins of the town, impregnable and unharmed. The heroic action of the inhabitants attracted admiration far and wide, and led to a wave of Norwegian patriotism, which was later recorded by Bjørnstjerne Bjørnson, the national poet of the nineteenth century, in the Norwegian national anthem:

So we preferred to burn our country
rather than let it fall,

remember what happened
at Fredrikshald!

At the Peace of Roskilde in 1658 the king of Denmark-Norway had had to cede the counties of Trøndelag in the north and Bohuslän in the south to Sweden, which meant that the then very modest fortress at Fredrikshald, which up to that time had been protected by the great castle of Bohus, now marked the south-eastern frontier of Norway. Within a year Fredrikshald was under attack from the east, but the cannon were able to repel the invaders. The fortress was immediately strengthened and reinforced, and in February 1659 the enemy made their expected return. The Swedish strategy was to mount an attack across the frozen waters of the Iddefjord, but they were forced back across the ice, which only just held. The people of Fredrikshald are supposed to have made holes in the ice and pushed their fallen enemies through, and even in 1727 it was said that at low tide one could see the skulls and bones lying at the bottom of the fjord.

A year after this ignominious retreat, in January 1660, the Swedish king again sent an army to invade Norway. The winter was a hard one; ma-

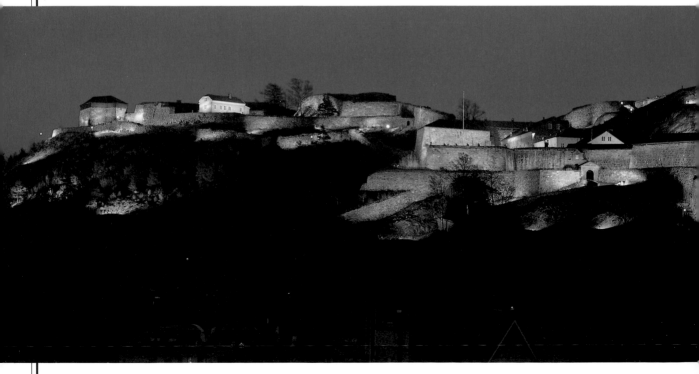

ny riders were said to have frozen to death on their horses; and the ice was thick, making it difficult for the Norwegians to break it up. But then the weather suddenly changed, melting the ice and creating difficulties for the Swedish army. The Norwegians took heart, and when the message came that King Charles X Gustav of Sweden had died, the Swedes were again forced to beat a retreat.

After these dramatic events it became obvious that Fredrikshald occupied a strategic position in relation to Sweden, and the building of a strong defensive fortress began in 1661. A large part of the huge quantities of stone that went into the walls and ramparts had to be carried by the local farmers, who were drafted in to help the soldiers. Fortunately the castle was completed by 1680, because it was a long time before the Swedes gave up their designs on this part of Norway.

As mentioned above, Charles XII had been driven back in 1716, but the warrior king, who had already waged war against the mighty Peter the Great of Russia, returned to the fray in November 1718, perhaps in an attempt to turn the tide of events, which was beginning to go

against Sweden. The king laid siege to Fredriksten with an enormous army, and on Sunday 11 December he planned to storm the castle walls. But again, fate intervened to protect the Norwegians. The evening before, Charles climbed up onto the breastworks thrown up in front of the forward trenches in order to oversee the preparations for the next day, when a single bullet came out of the blue and killed him outright. The officers tried to keep his death a secret and continue the siege, but rumours flew, and the very next day the siege was lifted and the army had to make its long and ignominious way home.

Peace reigned at Fredriksten until 1814, when the castle finally fell into enemy hands after a two-week-long siege. It was not taken by force, however, but as a result of negotiation. After the dissolution of the union with Sweden in 1905 it lost its military importance and the garrison was closed down.

There was always plenty going on at the castle, however, even in peacetime. Quarters were built, simple ones for the large numbers of men that the castle often had to accommodate, more comfortable ones for the officers and comparatively luxurious ones in the house of the commander of the garrison. As was usual for fortresses at that time, there were also slave quarters for prisoners; those at Fredriksten were the largest in the country after Akershus Castle.

In those days it was customary for soldiers to supply their own food, but they were given daily rations of bread and 2.6 litres of small beer. At the end of the seventeenth century a combined bakery and brewery was built, probably the oldest of its kind in Norway. It was able to supply 5000 men with bread, and brewed 2000 to 3000 litres of beer a day.

Today the most warlike activity at the castle is that of the military band, which still plays regularly. The castle is open to visitors, of which it receives thousands every year, including large numbers of erstwhile enemies from over the border.

HOLMENKOLLEN SKI JUMP AND THE SKI MUSEUM

Holmenkollen occupies a special place in the hearts of the people of Oslo. In a country like Norway, with its harsh climate, where a living had to be wrested from the soil and life depended precariously on the seasons, physical hardiness was necessarily a much admired quality, and skiing and all forms of winter sports rapidly became an important part of popular culture. Thus, when the newly erected Holmenkollen Ski Jump was opened on 31 January 1892, the whole of Oslo, some 20,000 strong, turned out to watch the first ski-jumping competition ever held there.

Holmenkollen replaced an older, smaller jump, Husebybakken, which had been built closer to Oslo. Unfortunately the snow conditions here were poorer. Holmenkollen was an ideal site; the only difficulty was that it was so hard to get to. There were no roads, and few people came up there. The idea of constructing a jump in this area came from the director of roads, Hans Krag, an enthusiastic skier and hiker who knew the country well. One warm summer's day in 1884 he took the mayor of Oslo for a brisk walk up the mountainside, and when they reached the top, Krag tied a handkerchief over the mayor's eyes, spun him round three times, and removed the handkerchief. At this time very few people were aware of the breathtaking view to be had from the heights of Holmenkollen, with the panorama of city and fjord spread out below, and the mayor was struck completely speechless. When he had got his breath back, he turned to Krag and offered him 5000 kroner to build a road up the mountainside, opening the way for what was to become one of the most fashionable suburbs of Oslo. A statue of Krag now stands at the view point above the present Holmenkollen arena.

When the time came to build a new ski jump to replace Husebybakken, Krag persuaded the authorities to build it on the eastern slope of the hill, running down to Besserudtjernet. This pool, fed by the surrounding marshland, is drained in the winter and forms the foot of the jump, but in the summer it is used for bathing. The jump was fairly simple at first but has since been added to, often in the teeth of opposition from traditionalists. When, in 1913, a 10 metre-high tower was added to give it height, many people felt that the limit had been reached. But improvements have continued to be made, the most recent being in connection with the World Cup that was held there in 1982.

Holmenkollen Sunday is Norway's second national day. The ski-jumping competition held here on the second Sunday in March is an annual event, attended by the international ski-jumping élite. Thousands of spectators stream up the mountainside, most of them having either parked their cars well away from the jump or taken the little wooden train to the nearest station. There is always a festival atmosphere, with booths selling hot drinks, snacks, and pieces of styrofoam to keep off the cold of the icy stone benches. The crowds are in high spirits and prepared to enjoy themselves. The Norwegian flag is everywhere, waving from fists, sticking out of rucksacks, painted on faces, and in the pattern formed by massed children's choirs dressed in red, white and blue uniforms ranged along the sides of the jump. The singing, the crowds, and the music combine to give the impression, on a sunny day, that the competitors are sailing through the air from sheer joie de vivre rather than for any competitive reasons.

The area round the jump is also used for cross-country skiing, and training and events are arranged here throughout the winter. In the summer concerts and other events are often held by the pool in the long light summer evenings.

The Holmenkollen ski jump has the highest number of visitors of any tourist attraction in Norway. The tower, which rises 412 metres over sea level, can be visited for the view it gives over

the city and the fjord. The actual jump consists of a three-storied building containing among other things a restaurant.

The Ski Museum, situated in the mountainside beside the ski jump, is the oldest in the world, and shows the development and practice of skiing through the ages. The oldest exhibit is a pair of skis that are 2500 years old. The polar explorers and their equipment occupy an important place, and souvenirs of the late King Olav V, who was a faithful supporter of all kinds of skiing and even took part in the Holmenkollen competition two years running, in 1922 and 1923. One of the best known stories about the king was the time he took the train up to Holmenkollen during the oil crisis of 1974, along with everybody else. His seat on the train is one of the exhibits, and a statue of the king, accompanied by his poodle, Troll, stands on the other side of the jump.

"His glance nailed me fast, and the fact that I did not fall apart each time he looked at me was because I was so terrified at the thought of the next second, when I would again have those frightening eyes on my face ... I felt like a corpse, and he like a hyena, untiring, bowed over me with arched back; his eyes, all-devouring, never satisfied." The dramatist, essayist and theatre producer Gunnar Heiberg was describing what it was like to sit for Gustav Vigeland.

And "all-devouring" and "never satisfied" were apt descriptions of Vigeland's attitude to his work and its demands. No other Norwegian artist, and few foreign ones, can ever have received such preferential treatment: in return for the right of ownership to most of his work, the Oslo municipal council gave Vigeland a house, an atelier, and an entire park in which to express himself. This was after Vigeland had refused a number of central and prestigious sites for his work on the grounds that they were too small.

The first sculpture that Vigeland designed for the park was the fountain, a giant bowl support-

ed on the shoulders of a group of men, later supplemented by a group of 16 statues representing the different phases of life which now stand around the edge of the fountain. The sketch was submit-

ted to the municipality of Oslo in the 1890s, and was greeted with enthusiasm; the poet and writer Bjørnstjerne Bjørnson, who had enormous influence during his lifetime, immediately proclaimed the young sculptor a genius. The final

result was the Vigeland Park: a series of bronze and granite sculptures consisting of about 650 figures, positioned along an avenue nearly a kilometre long, leading from the great wrought-iron gates in the east to the sundial and the Wheel of Life in the west. The theme is the evolution of man and the union of sculpture with Nature; Vigeland is depicting all aspects of man as he sees him, from fetal life to old age, in a style that is both monumental and generalized.

The progress of the work was carried on in an atmosphere of scandal and controversy; many people, and many artists, considered the entire project a waste of money and effort. It was begun during the 1920s and was not completed until after the Second World War, and the day it was finally finished, "we all woke up with an appalling hangover", wrote the art critic Øistein Parmann. He praised parts of the work but claimed that much of it merely showed that Vi-

tists in Norway, Vigeland won several scholarships, which allowed him to travel to Copenhagen, Paris, and Italy, where he was able to see the works of modern sculptors like Rodin as well as renaissance and classical sculpture. He remained deeply influenced by classical art and by the art of the ancient Egyptians.

Although the park is one of Oslo's greatest tourist attractions, and never fails to stir the imagination, much of Vigeland's best work was done early in life, and is not in the park at all. When one follows the artist's marathon run down the one kilometre-long avenue of sculptures, it is difficult not to feel that here he has turned his back on the best in himself. It does not really compare with the statue of Camilla Collett or the monument to Niels Henrik Abel in the gardens of the Royal Palace, or his works as a young man, which can be seen in Nasjonalgalleriet.

And yet the park never fails to impress, by its sheer size, by its evidence of one man's obsession with his own thoughts, by its completeness. Another feature is its accessibility; there are no notices saying "Keep off the grass", no prohibitions against bathing in the fountain, picnicking on the lawns, or touching, stroking or climbing on the statues. This is a park to enjoy with all the senses, and when one has climbed all the steps, and run one's hand over smooth warm granite skin, and admired the staggering size of the Monolith, and fed all the ducks, one can relax on a boat on the lake or visit the open-air restaurant that serves such delicious open sandwiches and cold drinks.

geland had expressed all he had to say at an early stage and for the rest was fuelled by brain and will power alone.

Vigeland's rise to fame was mainly due to his own efforts. He was born in Mandal, a very puritan small town on the south coast, in 1869, the son of a farmer. His childhood cannot have been happy; his father used to rip the covers off his bed every Good Friday in order to beat him. He started his career by carving in wood, and educated himself by drawing and by studying anatomy from books. At the age of 19 he showed his drawings to Brynjulf Bergslien, a neo-classical sculptor who had made his name, among other things, with the statue of Carl Johan in front of the royal Palace in Oslo. Bergslien found him so promising that he helped him to train further and allowed him to work in his studio. After his work had been accepted by the Autumn Exhibition, which is held every year and open to all ar-

THE MUNCH MUSEUM

"My pictures are my diaries," wrote Edvard Munch. This statement provides a unique insight into Munch's art. He made no attempt to paint anything other than his own subjective impressions; indeed, he poured scorn on any artist who tried to imitate objective reality. The majority of his paintings are to be found in the Munch Museum, which has hung them chronologically, so that the visitor can read his diary in the order in which it was "written", from the first fumblings of youth to the masterly grasp of imagery he exhibited during his last years.

Sixty-six years separate *Haakon Jarl's Death* by the 14-year-old boy from *Self portrait in coloured chalks* by the almost 80-year-old master. It was not a coincidence that the 14-year-old chose death as his theme; Munch's youth was dogged by death and tragedy. His mother died when he was only five, of the dreaded tuberculosis, and when he was 14 his older sister Sophie died of the same disease. His paintings express death again and again, *Death in the sickroom, The*

dead mother and the child, The sick child, The death struggle [he returned to the last theme later in a lithograph]. And although his childhood was not deprived of love or mental stimulation – his father was a doctor and a man of "considerable education and culture" – "pale little Edvard", as his mother called him

in her last letter before her death, never escaped the sadness of those early deaths. In later years he admitted that "Disease, madness and death were the dark angels that stood guard over my cradle, and have followed me ever since."

In the Munch Museum we can follow the pages of Munch's diary, from the bohemian life in

turn-of-the-century Christiania, while his "ideas matured", and resulted in works like *The morning after, Puberty*, and *Heredity*, through the decisive years when he painted *The vampire, Madonna, The scream*, up to what is perhaps his greatest "poem about life, love, and death", which he called *Life frieze*. Along with his increasing fame, his paintings reveal his crises, his neuroses, and his problems with alcohol. His ability to work, however, was unaffected by crises or alcohol, as we can see in his great wall paintings in the University auditorium, the Aula, and in pictures like *Night of stars, Model by a basket chair*, and *On the veranda*. By the time we reach the last pages of his "diary", the whole world had long recognized his genius. During these last years his sight had begun to fail, but not his strength or his pace of work. His last works are a celebration of life, painted in bold, daring colours, the work of a master who continued to develop right up to his death on 23 January 1944, at the age of 80.

"If my paintings are placed in a museum where other artists' works are also hung, their fate will depend on the taste of future generations. The museum might have a director or a board that did not like [my paintings]. They might be sold or, even worse, they might be relegated to the attic."

In order to protect his pictures, or his "children", as he called them, from such a terrible fate, Munch left all his works to the municipality of Oslo in his will.

Munch did not like to see his "children" leaving home, and parted with his paintings with a heavy heart. Nor did he sell very many of them:

"At first I received so little for my pictures that there was no point in selling them, and now I receive so much that I do not need to sell many."

Thus, at his death in 1944, the majority of Munch's most important works were still in his possession. His donation to the municipality amounted to about 1111 paintings, 12 sculptures, 18,162 prints covering about 818 subjects, about 3000 drawings, and a number of sketchbooks, printing plates, letters, notebooks, and the like.

At first the location of the Munch Museum at Tøyen met with strong opposition, since it was considered too far from the centre of town. However, since the museum, which was designed by Gunnar Fougner and Einar Myklebust, opened in 1963, the figures have put such considerations to shame. Munch's dramatic, soul-searching works have a universal appeal that transcends age and nationality.

The Museum also puts on concerts, readings, performances of children's theatre, lectures, films, and guided tours. Special exhibitions are arranged in the basement, often of the works of Munch's contemporaries, or of Munch's own studies and sketches, illustrating his development as an artist.

AKERSHUS CASTLE

"... were forced to retreat." These words form a proud refrain throughout the history of Akershus Castle. During the years from 1309 to 1716 nine commanders tried to take the castle, ranging from Duke Erik of Södermanland to Charles XII of Sweden, but all of them "were forced to retreat".

Akershus Castle was built by King Haakon V Magnusson in 1299, ostensibly to protect the town from Duke Erik of Södermanland, in Sweden. The fortress was solidly constructed and well protected, and when Duke Erik came knocking on the door nine years later, he was unsuccessful. However, since the town was actually situated on the other side of Bjørvika bay, and thus open to an enemy on the landward side, it is possible that the king's intention was more personal; he may have wanted to build a refuge for himself in times of trouble. Christian IV solved this problem by bringing the town to the castle; after the great fire of 1624 in which much of Oslo was burned down, he simply gave orders that the new town be built under the walls of Akershus.

During the whole of the seventeenth century the building of the town, which was rechristened

Christiania, and the renovation and alteration of the castle went on. This period has been called "the most intimate phase" of the union between the castle and the town. The medieval fortress was transformed to a renaissance palace, and the solidity of the walls was lightened by the graceful spire of the Blue Tower. The widespread use of cannon in the seventeenth century also made it necessary to fortify the castle against attack by artillery, and ramparts and bastions were constructed and further extended during the following century.

After the union with Sweden in 1814, the military activities were gradually decreased, and the grass-grown ramparts became a popular promenade where the citizens of the town would stroll of a summer evening, while swimming and, in the winter, skating, went on below the walls. It remained a landmark in relation to the capital; its ramparts and towers continued to rise above the modest two- and three-storied houses of the town.

A more serious side to the castle was its use as a prison at various times. The prisoners were known as "slaves", and put to work; Clarke in his *Travels in Scandinavia* tells how he visited the castle and watched them working in 1799. He also mentions the splendid view from the castle walls, and how the bay was so surrounded by land masses that it looked like a great lake scattered with islands and surrounded by blue mountains. The most famous prisoner to be incarcerated in the castle was the legendary Gjest Baardsen, a sort of Norwegian Robin Hood, who lived from 1791 to 1849. He was arrested and imprisoned an untold number of times, but always managed to escape, except from Akershus, the only prison which could hold him. During his enforced stays in prison he wiled away the time by writing among other things his memoirs, which have since been filmed.

The castle buildings have undergone many changes over the years, some due to fire, others to rebuilding and alterations. At the beginning of the present century it was in such a bad state of repair that many people wanted it pulled down,

among them the painter Christian Krohg: "Akers-hus Castle should be pulled down and replaced by a row of large commercial buildings. This would show the true face of Kristiania, the face of commerce and shipping." Fortunately the authorities decided to ignore him, and started a comprehensive work of restoration, begun under the leadership of the architects H. Sinding-Larsen and Arnstein Arneberg, which continued up to 1963.

And the castle has not lost its historic importance. It was the site of some of the most dramatic events in recent Norwegian history. On 9 June 1905 Norway's secession from Sweden was marked by the raising of the new Norwegian flag on the King's Battery. It was at Akershus Castle on 1 February 1942 that Vidkun Quisling signed the document appointing him Minister President of Norway under German occupation. Political prisoners were interned in the castle during the war, and after it Norwegian collabor-

ators were housed there. Over 40 resistance workers were executed in the main square in front of the castle, and here Pope John Paul II, the first pope ever to visit Norway, officiated at an outdoor mass on 1 June 1989.

The castle now houses several museums and is also used for state occasions and official entertainments. The Resistance Museum gives an excellent picture of Norway under the Occupation, and of course the castle itself can be visited, with the help of guides in national costume. The crypt below the chapel of Slottskirken contains the Royal Mausoleum.

THE FOLK MUSEUM

By the end of the nineteenth century, preserving the fast disappearing peasant culture of Norway was becoming a matter of urgency. The isolated valleys, which had developed individually over the centuries, were being overtaken by progress, and age-old traditions were being replaced by an industrialized culture. There were other reasons, too, why the national romantic movement was particularly strong in Norway at this time. The country had just achieved its own constitution after 400 years of Danish rule, and although

it was joined in a union with Sweden under a common king, it was in the process of building up its own national institutions and feeling, for the first time for hundreds of years, like an independent nation. Thus it was not a coincidence that in 1894 the young Hans Aall founded a folk museum to try to preserve the last traces of the peasant and popular culture that was so characteristic of Norway. The museum was modelled on the Skansen Museum in Stockholm, an open-air museum that would show furniture and objects of daily use displayed in their natural surroundings and not in glass cases with labels attached. The original houses were taken apart and the logs carefully numbered, then they were reassembled on their new sites in the museum.

The first house to be transported to the new

museum was Raulandsstua, from Telemark, which was built in about 1300 and is one of the few remaining houses from the Middle Ages in the country. Most of the farms and buildings in the museum date from the end of the sixteenth to the middle of the nineteenth centuries, but the building methods show little development – the art of building in wood for maximum warmth and protection from the weather was developed early on and had little reason to change. One of the most influential developments was not in the external architecture at all; it was the invention of the built-in fireplace with a chimney, which could be placed in a corner of the room, freeing the middle of the floor and protecting the inhabitants from the problems of perpetual smoke.

Architectonic differences are found, not so much over time as between regions. The farm from Hardanger, on the west coast of Norway, shows that the notched log buildings of eastern Norway and the central valleys have given way to horizontal cladding, and continuing on to the farms from the storm-tossed south-west coast of Jæren, the houses become lower and lower, huddling into the ground to create as little resistance as possible to the wind. The same differences can be seen in the roofing materials, which vary from inland turf, excellent insulation against snow, to the stone slates from the flinty treeless country around Stavanger. Thus the visitor can in one afternoon experience the whole of southern and central Norway compressed into about 140 decares of natural countryside, comparing the different types of regional architecture, and, during the summer, entering the homes of farmers, merchants, and labourers to see how they used to live. On Sundays mass is held in the beautiful thirteenth-century stave church from Gol in Halling-

dal, Roman Catholic and Lutheran services being held on alternate Sundays. Although much of the exterior has been restored, the interior and the main structural elements are original. There is a thirteenth-century pew originally from Heddal Stave Church, with carvings showing motifs from Norwegian history, and the painted decorations in the choir and apse were done in 1652.

After touring the countryside, the visitor may turn to "Gamlebyen", a reconstruction of nineteenth-century Christiania, as Oslo used to be called. Here, too, the buildings are original; they have been carefully transported from their original sites and reassembled. Small early nineteenth-century workers' houses of wood from the suburb of Enerhaugen, where mother, father, and a large brood of children lived in one room and kitchen, existed side by side with the houses of the more affluent, like Collett-Cappelen House, an elegant seventeenth-century structure in half-timbered brick. Next door to this is the old prison, and further on are workshops, offices, and a chemist shop. Potters and silversmiths still produce their wares by the old methods, and at the grocer's they sell old-fashioned sugary sweets in tempting colours.

In addition to the open-air museum there are two large buildings with more conventional collections of furniture, glass and porcelain, examples of rose painting and woodcarving, national costumes and handwoven textiles, musical instruments, and not least a large collection of post-Reformation church furnishings and other objects. Also on view are Henrik Ibsen's study, where he wrote so many of his plays, and the first assembly room of the Norwegian Storting, or parliament, which met in the Oslo Cathedral School until 1854.

Activities are arranged at the Folk Museum all the year round. Midsummer's Eve is celebrated in the traditional way, with dancing and a huge bonfire; in the autumn there is sheepshearing and demonstrations of carding and spinning, and on the first Sunday in Advent every year a Christmas market is held.

THE MARITIME MUSEUM

From the outside the museum rises above the water like the prow of a ship, and inside only a sheet of glass separates you from the fjord. The building was designed by Trond Eliassen and Birger Lambertz-Nilssen and was only completed in 1974; before that the museum was housed in a boathouse, which the collection shared with the polar vessel *Fram*.

Norway's long Atlantic seaboard, her convoluted coastline, scattered with islands and intersected with fjords, and her lack of large tracts of arable land for farming, have all contributed to make her pre-eminently a maritime nation. Her transport routes, even from one part of the country to another, have been mainly along waterways, from fjord to fjord and along rivers and inland lakes. Owing to the mountainous nature of the country, the coastal population of Norway had to become seafarers and fishermen, and in earlier times, when the Vikings developed their wonderful longships, raiders and colonizers too. Because of her isolated position, however, Norway could not become a trading centre, and it was not until the end of the eighteenth century that she began to acquire a large commercial fleet. At this time the Dutch supremacy at sea had declined and England, another maritime nation, was at war. From this propitious start the commercial fleet was built up throughout the nineteenth century and the shipping industry has been a very important part of Norwegian commercial life ever since.

The Maritime Museum shows all aspects of sea and water-borne traffic and industries, of which Norway has a great variety. Fishing, whaling, coastal trade and communications, the lighthouse service, the rescue services, and not least polar exploration, are all featured. Daily life on board ship is shown, and the art of boat-building is illustrated by the many different types of vessels, each designed for a special purpose, which are displayed in the two-storied hall.

Down by the water is the *Gjøa*, the vessel in which Roald Amundsen sailed through the North-West Passage in 1903–06, and moored nearby is *Svanen*, the Swan, a three-masted topsail schooner used for demonstration purposes and travelling exhibitions.

THE FRAM MUSEUM

Standing in its own triangular building is probably the most famous vessel in the history of polar exploration, the three-masted schooner *Fram*. Fridtjof Nansen had the *Fram* built by Colin Archer to a special design that would enable her to withstand the screwing action of the ice, which can crush a normal hull. Thus the hull was made of three shells, the innermost of oak, and the outer ones of an even harder wood, and the propeller and rudder could be hoisted up out of the way of the ice. Nansen's plan was to let the ship freeze fast in the ice off the coast of Siberia. It would then drift with the current, which he had calculated would run north-west and eventually reach the North Pole. In this he was partly right; the current did indeed run north-west, but not far north enough, and Nansen and Hjalmar Johansen left the ship and struck out on their own to try and find the Pole. Although they had to give up, they had travelled further north than anyone else at that time, and Nansen's theory of the current was also shown to be correct in principle, since the *Fram* had drifted north of Svalbard by the time she was finally set free from the ice, the following spring.

The *Fram* was used for two more expeditions. The first was in 1898–1902 and was led by Otto Sverdrup. The expedition intended to sail north over Greenland, but the ice was too thick, and instead the *Fram* was anchored off the coast and served as a base for inland expeditions.

Having sailed further north than any other ship before her, the *Fram* was finally destined to sail further south as well. Roald Amundsen set out in the *Fram* in 1910, ostensibly for the North Pole. However, off Madeira, the last possible port of call, he announced his plans to an astonished world, and turned south before anyone could prevent him. The *Fram* was anchored in Hvalbukta and used for collecting scientific material while Amundsen and his four companions made their successful journey to the South Pole.

THE KON-TIKI MUSEUM

Who has not heard of Thor Heyerdahl, seafarer and adventurer, man of ideas and man of action, a visionary who not only formed new theories about the transport routes of ancient peoples, but who also risked his own life to test them.

For it was undoubtedly a risk to construct a raft of balsa wood and sail it 8000 kilometres across the Pacific, well out of reach of land and any possible outside help. The raft was based on the designs of ancient balsa rafts in Ecuador and Peru and consisted of nine logs of balsa wood bound together with creepers and equipped with a mast, sail, centreboards, a rudder, and a bamboo hut with a roof of plaited banana leaves. It was called after the hero of an Indian legend, whose face appears on the sail. Kon-Tiki was a heroic figure who mediated between the Indians of Peru and the sun, the mightiest of the gods. Kon-Tiki escaped from his enemies by sailing into the sunset on a balsa wood raft. In Polynesia Tiki is a god, the greatest of them all, the son of the sun, and he led his people out into the Pacific. Heyerdahl and six companions, five Norwegians and a Swede, proved that it was at any rate

possible that the people of Peru could have sailed on their fragile rafts to the islands of Polynesia, a journey that took Heyerdahl and his crew 101 days, sailing from Callao in Peru to Roroia in Polynesia.

The voyage of the Kon-Tiki attracted worldwide attention, and in the natural course of things it also attracted scientific criticism. Sir Peter Bucks, the leading authority on Polynesia and himself half Maori, said that while it was no doubt an adventure, one could hardly call it a scientific expedition. Another expert accused Heyerdahl of faking the expedition, and a third proposed that the whole thing should be ignored. More recent finds, however, during another expedition by Heyerdahl to the Galapagos Islands, have supported his theory.

Heyerdahl's next idea was to investigate Easter Island, which, in spite of its intriguing culture, had been almost completely neglected by archaeologists. The origin of the enormous stone statues, and the mystery of how they were transported and placed upright, have since been studied and solved, but Heyerdahl was among the first to be interested in the question, and on his expedition there in 1955–56 he found links with South American Indian culture, on this island 4000 kilometres from the nearest land. In the volcanic craters of the island he also found totora reeds growing, which had been cultivated and used by the Incas of Peru, among other things to build their reed boats.

The Ra expeditions, in 1969 and 1970, were undertaken to show that it was possible to cross the Atlantic in reed boats, and that men from the ancient African and Egyptian civilizations could have done so and taken their culture with them to America. The Ra II, made of papyrus, crossed the Atlantic in 57 days, leaving Safi in Morocco and sailing 6000 kilometres over the open sea to land in Barbados, with eight men from eight nations on board. In addition to investigating cultural links, Heyerdahl was always keen to foster international cooperation.

In November 1977 Heyerdahl set out on another expedition, which was less successful.

This was to test another type of reed boat, this time called the *Tigris*. It set out from Iraq, but ended in Djibouti five months later, a victim of lack of international cooperation. Although the *Tigris* carried the United Nations flag, she was refused entry to many of the Red Sea ports because of fighting, and Heyerdahl finally set fire to her in protest.

The Kon-Tiki Museum contains the original famous raft in its lifelike setting, an artifical aquarium with a model of the fearsome whale shark, manuscripts and diaries written by Heyerdahl and his companions on the various voyages, and exhibits from Easter Island. Among these are the only existing copy of a 9.2 metre-high Easter Island statue, and various original sculptures. There is also a section on the Ra expeditions, and a research centre with a well-stocked library.

THE VIKING SHIP MUSEUM

Was it the invention of the keel that made the Viking ships so eminently seaworthy? At any rate it was the design of their longships – broad and low in the water, but easily manoeuvrable – that enabled them to carry out their long voyages and raid, plunder, and trade with impunity up and down the coast of Europe.

Although they were so admirably adapted for

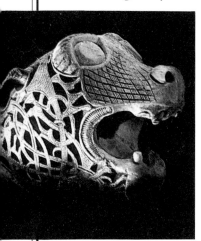

seafaring, the Viking ships were anything but luxurious. Each man had a chest for his possessions, but everything else had to be placed on the open deck. The crew ate and slept where they sat, and their only protection from the weather was a canvass sail. The sun and the stars were used for navigation, and in cloudy weather they used a primitive direction-finding device, although in some sagas reference is made to an instrument called a "sun-stone" – perhaps the forerunner of a compass?

The Vikings were customarily buried in boats. A burial chamber was constructed in the ship's stern, and in it were placed the dead man or woman along with favourite animals, horses and dogs, useful articles and ornaments, and a supply of food and drink. This practice has provided a rich source of information about daily life in Viking times. The three ships in the Museum were all grave finds. The Tune ship was excavated on the eastern side of the Oslo fjord in 1867, and dates back to the second half of the ninth century. It is 20 metres long, 4 metres wide, and equipped with a sail and 11 or 12 pairs of oars. It was in a very bad state of repair,

however, and could be only partly restored.

The largest and best preserved of the ships is the Gokstad ship. It was found on the west side of the Oslo fjord in 1880, and dates back to about 850. This is a classical seagoing longship, 24 metres in length, with 16 pairs of oars for 32 rowers. When it was excavated, 64 shields hung along the gunwhales, covering the oar openings and making it impossible to row. It is now thought that the shields were hung there when the ship was in harbour and removed when the oars were used.

The Oseberg ship also has shields hung along the gunwhales, but in such a way that they do not obstruct the oars. This is the most richly decorated and ornamental of the ships, intended for sailing along the coast on pleasure trips. The remains of two women were found on board, who are thought to be Queen Aasa and her handmaiden. They were surrounded by objects, including beautifully decorated sledges and pieces of harness, household objects, tools and implements, leather shoes, specially made for swollen feet, textiles, jewels, and even small boats. The ship is 22 metres long and dates from the end of the ninth century.

According to the sagas, the Vikings camped on land when they could, and the remains of tents were found on board both the Gokstad and the Oseberg ship. The ships also contained the remains of a large handsome bed with carved posts, which probably served as a luxurious camp bed for the chief in charge of the expedition. The rest of the crew probably slept in double sleeping bags, which were used to store weapons and other articles during the day. It is not known what the diet on board was like, but cauldrons and other equipment for cooking over open fires have been

found. Their everyday diet probably consisted of dried fish and smoked or salted meat products, washed down with water, sour milk, and ale. The water was stored in leather bags, like those still used to store wine in Mediterranean countries.

The chariot in the Oseberg ship is the only wheeled vehicle from Viking times that has been found. Considering what the roads must have

been like, it is not surprising that the underside of the carriage is equipped with two stout handles so that it could be lifted up when it stuck and perhaps even carried over difficult ground. The rich decorations indicate that it was probably used by a woman of high rank.

The building that so dramatically accentuates the lines of the Viking ships was designed by Arnstein Arneberg and completed in 1954.

THE ROYAL BURIAL MOUNDS AT BORRE

North of Oseberg and Gokstad, where the two best preserved Viking ships were found, lies Borre, where the remains of many kings lie buried. The burial mounds lie in beautiful surroundings, with green and fertile meadows where large oak and beech trees grow in addition to the more usual birch. The site is now a national park, but when the mounds were first discovered, during the last century, it was church property.

The story of these burial mounds is a story of lost opportunities, for grave robbers and vandalism, combined with a total lack of interest in the past, meant that by the time it was realized what a rich potential the mounds represented, most of the contents had been destroyed. After the grave robbers came the Public Roads Administration, which in 1852 purchased the right to dig up one of the mounds and use the earth for road building. It was this which drew attention to the find, because the workers kept finding nails and other objects indicating that this was a ship grave. Rewards were offered, and in their enthusiasm the workers dug wildly, destroying many of the objects they were trying to uncover. All the mounds have been hacked about, and at least three of

them have been levelled, so that now there are only five and the remains of a sixth left. A further disadvantage was that they contained no blue clay, with its wonderful preserving proper-

ties, such as had kept the wood and textiles in the Gokstad and Oseberg finds from decaying.

In the wave of nationalism that swept Norway during the last century and that culminated in her emergence as an independent nation, the kings' graves at Borre came to be regarded as

ninth century, and according to Snorre Sturlason, the thirteenth-century author of the saga of the Ynglings, his forefathers were buried at Borre. This would mean that the earliest mounds date back to the beginning of the ninth century. However, historians now believe that the burial ground of the Ynglings is merely a legend, and the objects found at Borre have been dated to the end of the ninth century.

In Viking times the sea came much further inland, probably reaching the feet of the nearest mounds. The mounds measure about 50 metres in diameter and up to 6,5 metres in height, and are surrounded by moats that in Viking times were filled with water. A system of earthworks formed access bridges. When one of the smaller ones was excavated in 1927, it was found to contain very simply equipped graves from the Iron Age and the Viking period. But the most important find was the "Borre Find", in the mound dug into by the Public Roads Administration, and is one of the major finds from the Viking Age. Although it had been so badly desecrated, the finds that remained consisted of parts of a longship that was probably about 20 metres long, iron nails from the ship, bronze ornaments for harness and riding equipment, a few household objects, and a beautiful Frankish goblet made of glass. The harness ornaments, which are probably from the end of the ninth century, are important finds because they are examples of the "Borre style", which is characterized by a unique ribbon pattern known as the "ring chain" and ribbon knots and bows in high relief. This style succeeded the Oseberg style, being associated with approximately the second half of the ninth century, and other objects in the Borre style have been found in two high-ranking nobles' graves in Vestfold county, the Oseberg and the Gokstad finds, which are exhibited in the Viking Ship Museum.

the cradle of the Norwegian nation. For it was the kings of the Yngling dynasty that were supposed to lie buried there, and it was this dynasty, under Harald Fairhair, which was responsible for uniting Norway into one kingdom. Harald came to power during the second half of the

LYNGØR

The south coast is Norway's holiday coast. Scattered along it are idyllic fishing villages with sparkling white-painted houses and flower-filled gardens. The sun shines on the south coast; the sea is blue; there are excellent conditions for fishing and boating; and everyone who can afford it tries to have a holiday cottage here and to spend as much of the summer in it as possible. Here, in the summer, artists and writers gather, arts and crafts flourish, the population trebles, tourists abound. And one of the most idyllic villages of all is Lyngør.

Lyngør is not very big; although it consists of four islands, Holmen, Odden, Lyngørsida, and Steinsøya, its total population numbers only 110. But Lyngør has achieved success against heavy odds. It has succeeded in reversing the trend towards gradual depopulation that so many small communities are facing, and has managed to keep its shop, its school, its post office and its ferry. In 1991 it received the prize for Europe's best-kept village.

The four islands of Lyngør screen and protect the mainland from the worst of the weather, and not until the end of the sixteenth century is there mention of any permanent inhabitants in the

area. The earth is not fertile, nor was the fishing and hunting particularly good, so the population remained very small. In 1680 there were only three families, numbering 13 people, on the islands. By the beginning of the nineteenth century, however, the numbers had doubled, and by 1815 there were 200 people living there. Foreign ships had begun calling at ports along the whole south coast, taking on board exports which included timber, boats, flagstones, and lobsters.

The foreign captains were unused to the rock-studded waters off the coast, and local pilots were needed in large numbers to steer Dutch, Danish, and English captains safely through the difficult waters and between the islands. The Norwegian commercial fleet was also beginning to attain sizable proportions, and by 1767 it numbered 600 ships, 124 of which came from the small strip of coast between Risør and Arendal.

Being at this time united with Denmark, Norway was involved in the Napoleonic war, and in 1812 Lyngør itself became involved. Denmark-Norway had sided with France, and England had defeated the Danish-Norwegian fleet in 1807 and was in control of the northern waters. On 6 July there was a battle off Lyngør between the Danish-Norwegian frigate *Najaden* and the English warship the *Dictator*. The *Najaden* was sunk, and 127 of a crew of 315 lost their lives. A monument now commemorates them. During the war the English blockade of the North Sea prevented ships from reaching Norway with provisions, and hunger drove many of the local population in open boats to Denmark to buy corn. Many of them were captured by the English and spent the rest of the war in an English prison. One of these was a Lyngør man named Anders Olsen, but he managed to escape and returned home to become a successful merchant and shipowner.

Most of the old houses in Lyngør today were built between 1840 and the beginning of the present century. This was the heyday of the village, and in 1900 there were as many as 600 people living there. From the turn of the century, however, steamships began to supplant the sailing ships completely, leaving a trail of bankruptcies among the shipowners along the coast. Ships ceased to call at little outports like Lyngør, and went straight to the seat of trade instead, and the shipowning industries followed them.

The picture was not completely black, however. With the decline in one industry came the rise of another: tourism. The first tourists came to Lyngør by accident; they were a young couple on their honeymoon, who came for a few days

and spent the whole summer. The bride wrote down her impressions:

"These people are obviously very cultured, to judge by their articulate way of speaking and the order and cleanliness of the surroundings. They also seem to be wealthier than we had expected ... I am constantly meeting new surprises. Lyngør lies about 250 kilometres south of Christiania [Oslo], but the vegetation is amazingly lush; ivy grows wild, and everything is so beautiful and fruitful."

Two years later the first summer cottages were built, followed in the 1930s by a boarding house. The numbers of summer visitors and tourists grew, and the population declined steadily. By the 1970s the local inhabitants were so worried by the declining figures that they started a campaign to keep the local community alive. Not that they do not want the tourists. The village is full of attractions for visitors, with hotels, restaurants, historical walks, courses in diving, to name a few. But it is no longer possible to buy a house in Lyngør unless one intends to live there permanently.

KRISTIANSAND ZOO

The Norwegian woods are the last place one would expect to find camels and zebra and chimpanzees, but in fact camels do very well in the Norwegian climate. There is no long tradition of zoos in Norway, and the general population's lack of familiarity with exotic animals is shown by the following story. Shortly after the zoo first opened in 1964 a shipment of camels arrived at Kristiansand railway station one summer's day, bound for the zoo. The transport from the zoo was delayed, and the camels had to wait for some time in the sun before being collected. This provoked indignant letters to the local paper: People wished to call attention to the appalling cruelty to animals shown by the authorities in allowing these poor creatures to stand about in the hot sun for an absolutely scandalous number of hours without any protection!

But the camels thrived. Bactrian camels are found as far north as Siberia, and appear to enjoy both the pinewoods and the snow, where they can even give birth without any ill effects. The birth rate at the zoo is so high that at one time it was among the leading European exporters of camels to other zoos, even sending camels to Canada.

One of the aims of the zoo is the preservation and breeding of rare and threatened species. Thus it has an ordinary panda, a little reddish-brown animal from Asia, of which there are only about 1000 left in the wild, and only about 200 in zoos; the king python from South America, which has hatched out 19 babies; and the dwarf hippopotamus from Liberia, of which there are only about 400 left in the whole world,

and which have so far produced three offspring. The latest acquisition is a pair of Nordic wolves, which are very much a threatened species, and it is hoped that they too will thrive and breed here in their natural environment.

The darling of the zoo, its very own mascot, is of course Julius the chimpanzee. Julius was born in the zoo, but was rejected by his mother and brought up by the director of the zoo with his own small girls, before being successfully reintegrated with the other chimpanzees as an adolescent. The book about Julius' childhood has been a best-seller and is translated into nine languages, and the television film also enjoyed a huge success. Chimpanzees are also threatened in the wild, and it is hoped that Julius will produce lots of offspring, especially since a mate, Josefine, was found for him and imported from Sweden.

Adjoining the zoo is a large Amusement Park with a log flume, bobsleighs, roller coasters, bumper cars and a mini-train. There is treasure-hunting with pirates on board a real pirate ship called the *Klara*, children's theatre, a circus tent, and Summer Island, where there is a large swimming pool with water chutes.

Next door to the Amusement Park is a model of Torbjørn Egner's *The Singing Town*. The story of the Singing Town and its inhabitants has given pleasure to children in 24 different languages, and now it can be visited in real life, so to speak.

Egner himself made a model of the Singing Town, and in 1991 the full-scale town stood ready to welcome the first children, with its tram

and its 32 houses, surrounded by a wall. The
robbers' house is outside the gates of the town,
just as it should be.

Egner derived the inspiration for the Singing
Town from his journeys to the Mediterranean,
especially Morocco, but he never intended to re-
create a true copy of a Mediterranean town. The
Singing Town is meant to be naive, a town of
child-like simplicity with cobbled streets where
seals and hens, parrots, horses and camels roam,
and the plants have an exotic look. The houses
are all open and Tobias can be visited in his tower or one can call on Aunt Sophy or Chief
Constable Bastian, or even the robbers. After
that it is worth visiting the bakery for a cake and
a cold drink, or the butcher's for a hot dog.

HEDDAL STAVE CHURCH

Once upon a time there was a church that was built by a troll. The church was so large and so beautiful that people said it could not have been built by human hand. The story runs as follows.

When Norway was converted to Christianity, a group of farmers in Heddal decided to build a church in honour of the White Christ. One day a stranger approached one of the farmers, who was called Raud Rygi, and offered to build the church if Raud Rygi would comply with one of three conditions: he must fetch down the sun and the moon from heaven, he must let his heart's blood run, or he must find out the name of the stranger. Raud Rygi agreed to this, and the stranger started building. But soon Raud Rygi began to fear for his life, for the stranger built very fast indeed, and it was obvious that the church would be finished by the third day. And as he paced up and down on his farm, wondering what to do, he heard a deep and beautiful voice singing inside Svintryberget [the mountain southeast of the church]. The song went:

Hush, hush little child,
tomorrow comes Finn,
with the moon and the sun
and a Christian heart ...

Then Raud Rygi understood that the stranger was a mountain troll and that his name was Finn. On the third day the stranger came to Raud Rygi and said that the church was finished and he could come and take it. They went into the church, and Raud Rygi struck the main pillar in the middle of the church and said, "Finn, this is crooked." "And it can become even crookeder now," said Finn, and he ran out of the church and disappeared into the mountain.

But the wonder of the church has remained ever since. In 1595 Bishop Jens Nilssøn wrote after a visit: "Heiterdals [sic] Church is a wooden church, very strangely constructed with three small towers, one at the east end over the choir, one over the centre of the choir and one over the middle of the church, where the bells hang, and which is the largest." Professor Lorentz Dietrichson, the art historian, described it as "The richest and finest of the monuments of its kind", and one can well believe that such a church, so far outside the usual traditions of ecclesiastical architecture as we know it in Europe, and such a particularly large and interesting example of its kind, must have come from another world. Unlike many of the other stave churches, this one is not built on a rise, which would have made its proportions even more imposing, but on the flat bank of the river Heddøla, making it easy for the farmers who lived around the lake of Heddalsvatnet to come to church by boat.

The church is dedicated to the Virgin Mary, and was probably built in about 1250, in the reign of Haakon Haakonsson, a flourishing period of great activity in many spheres. Under this king, who reigned from about 1217 to 1263, a national style of art flourished in Norway, uninfluenced by European trends, which found expression in the stave churches and their decoration. Other types of art and architecture, such as painting, were influenced by the prevailing gothic. The date of the church has been established on the basis of a runic inscription on the fourth plank in the wall to the right of the entrance portal, and on the basis of the style of the carving on the portals, where plant tendrils are intertwined with the animal ornamentation. The first mention of the church, however, occurs in a document dated 1315. Like many of the stave churches, the Heddal church may well be built around an earlier building, since the choir is thought to have been the nave in a smaller church from the twelfth century.

Nor did Heddal church escape the zeal of the Reformation. In the mid-seventeenth century a low, flat ceiling with windows just beneath it was installed, and so it remained until about 1850, when the Danish architect Johan Henrik Nebelong removed the renaissance interior but without improving the church in any way; on the contrary, Nebelong's work was greeted with displeasure by his contemporaries. Another hundred years went by before any more restoration work was done, and then Gudolf Blakstad and Herman Munthe-Kaas returned the church to the condition it was in during the Middle Ages, revealing the main lines of the interior and many of the structural details. The remains of decorations from medieval times and from the seventeenth century were also discovered.

Not only the generous proportions, but also the richness of the furnishings originally in the church indicate that Norway at this time, and the district too, were experiencing a period of wealth and stability. Many of the furnishings are now displayed elsewhere, but the medieval chair in the choir is still there, and so is the altarpiece from 1667.

THE KONGSBERG SILVER MINE

One summer's day in 1623, two children who were out tending their families' herds discovered a lump of silver lying on the ground. They took it home and the families melted it down and made it into buttons and other small articles, which they tried to sell secretly. However, the story of the find came to the ears of the authorities, and the fathers were arrested; later the only thanks they got was poorly paid work in the silver mine.

This is one of the stories told about the discovery of the vein of silver in the hills near Kongsberg. Whatever the details, the find created a great sensation, and raised a furore of hopes and expectations of a rich future for the town. Within a year the crown had appropriated the property and issued a royal decree making it an offense to search for silver at the site of the discovery. Christian IV called the town Konningsberg [the King's Mountain), and the first mine was called Kongens Gruve [the King's Mine]. The first six tons of silver was transported at once to Copenhagen, where the Master of the Royal Mint, Nicolai Schwabe, made them into riksdaler. The king gave the first coins to be minted from Norwegian silver to his children,

and thanks were offered up in all the churches in Norway and Denmark for the find.

The miners used hammers and crowbars to hack their way into the mountain. Until the discovery of dynamite, heat was used to open up the rock face. Dried wood was piled against the mountainside and set alight; when the fire had burned long enough to heat the rock, the miners threw cold water over it so that it cracked. Thus their work proceeded by slow and painful degrees.

At first the search for the vein was haphazard; even water-divining rods were used. In 1624, however, contact was made with the Duke of Brunswick, whose territory included the mining district of Harz, and some 30 experts were sent north to prospect. Until about 1650 Germans were in a majority in the mine, and ever since have been frequently sent for when expert advice is needed.

The Kongsberg silver mine is the only place in the world where pure silver is found. Lumps of silver weighing up to 300 kilos had to be dragged up the deep shafts, a backbreaking task. A drum of steel wire was installed which was kept revolving by a horse walking in a circle, and by this system weights could be raised from 100 metres underground, but as the tunnels into the mountainside grew deeper even this method failed to solve the transport problem. The mine was about to shut down completely, when German expertise again came to the rescue, in the form of Heinrich Schlanbusch, who had a wide experience of silver mines and coin-minting. Schlanbusch recommended the use of a water wheel, and a complex system of artificial dams and gutters for collecting water was set up. The network of pipelines covered the whole mountain, and drove a system of water-wheels and crushing plants which was considered to be one of the most advanced in Europe.

In 1770 Kongsberg was the largest town in Norway, with eight thousand inhabitants, half of whom worked in the mine. It was gruelling work. The workers' instructions of 1724 laid down that the miners had to meet up at Kirketorvet at 4 o'clock in the morning and march to their respective mines, where after a short prayer they descended the long ladders by the weak light of tallow candles. The tunnels were cold, damp and smoky in spite of the ventilation shafts that were supposed to clear the worst of the

smoke from the fires. Children were also part of the work force, and by the age of 40 a miner was usually completely worn out.

After the end of the eighteenth century the output began to decline, and in 1805 the king closed it down. This resulted in great poverty and misery among the townspeople, which was aggravated by the terrible town fire of 1810. In 1816, however, an attempt was made to re-open the mine, and a large find in 1830 led to a resurgence of activity until 1862. Since then the profits have decreased steadily, and in 1957 the Silver Mine was shut down for good. During the course of its 334 years of history, the mine has produced about 1500 tons of pure silver.

Today a small train takes visitors round the mine, along a 2.3 kilometre track that descends 342 metres below sea level. The furnace house, which was built in 1842 in the town itself, has been turned into a museum. It shows the various phases of the mining process, and contains exhibitions of minerals, coins and medals, and lumps of silver, some of it twisted into strange and beautiful natural shapes.

HE INDUSTRIAL WORKERS' MUSEUM AT VEMORK

The heroes of Telemark – the sabotage of the heavy water plant during the Second World War carried out by these brave men has been the subject of several books and films, and still stands out as one of the most important actions of the Norwegian resistance. The objective was to stop the German production of heavy water, which is an essential ingredient in the making of an atomic bomb.

The first sabotage was attempted by British planes in November 1942, but it misfired. The task was then given to Linge Company, a commando troop in the Norwegian army stationed in Scotland. On 16 February 1943 a group of specially trained young Norwegians landed on Hardangervidda, 50 kilometres from their target. In spite of being caught in a terrible storm, they finally managed to make contact with the secret radio station manned by their comrades, and on the evening of 27 February everything was ready. Their plan was extremely daring, but it worked, and as a result the production equipment in front of Vemork power plant was blown up. The saboteurs managed to get out before the explosion and make their getaway without anyone being either killed or captured, although 3000 Germans combed Hardangervidda for a long time afterwards.

However, heavy water was extremely important to the Germans, and they succeeded in rebuilding the production plant. The Americans were so concerned that they decided to interfere, and on 16 November 1943, 160 Flying Fortresses came flying in over Rjukan and dropped 400 tons of bombs. This time the Germans gave up their plans for continuing production at Vemork, and decided to transport what they had saved from the bombing to Germany. London sent an urgent message; this transport *had* to be

stopped. On 20 February 1944 a time bomb exploded on the ferryboat *Hydro*, which went to the bottom of Tinnsjøen with a full cargo of potash. The fight to stop the production of heavy water was over, but it had cost 91 lives.

But Vemork is more than an incident in Norwegian military history; it is highly representative of Norwegian industrial history as well. At the beginning of the present century two Norwegians, Kristian Birkeland and Sam Eyde, discovered a method of extracting nitrogen from air, and created the foundations for a major industry. For the method enabled inorganic fertilizer to be produced on a large scale, which revolutionized agriculture and the world's food production. This was the method that formed the starting point for the firm of Norsk Hydro, now a major industrial concern, in 1905.

The extraction method required a plentiful supply of cheap water power, and the far-sighted Eyde made sure of this by building a plant beside the Rjukan falls. Within a short time the peaceful agricultural community in Vestfjorddalen was transformed into an industrial society

– a town grew up around the falls, and in 20 years the population had swelled to six time the size. Yet although this small inward-looking farming community had become a modern town in record time, the transformation was accomplished gracefully, and the result was unusually attractive, thanks to the efforts of several major contemporary architects.

After the first Klondyke rush, the town settled down and developed a strong working-class culture, and it is this among other things that the Industrial Workers' Museum seeks to show. The Museum, which was opened in 1988, is housed in the power station that was built between 1907

and 1911. When it opened it was the largest in the world, and it continued to operate until 1971. Its architectonic quality, however, was so high that it was decided to preserve it, and in 1975 Norsk Hydro was required by the Ministry of Industry to maintain the building together with its machinery and penstock.

The section of the museum dealing with electricity and energy spans the past and the future. It illustrates the industrial progress from the earliest development of watercourses up to the present day and even the future – there is a special exhibition of alternative sources of energy, with a newly developed heat pump that utilizes

the heat produced by the cooling water used for New Vemork. A small-scale model with its own waterfall demonstrates how a power station works.

A separate exhibition of social history shows the development of industrialization and the trade union movement since the beginning of the century. It emphasizes the influence that trade unions have had in shaping modern society in general, and the place occupied by industrial workers in the local community in particular. Finally, a separate section of the museum is devoted to the exploits of the heroes of Telemark, and the events of the war.

OLD STAVANGER

It was fortunate for the old town in Stavanger that the national and local economic situation in the second half of the 1940s was so bad. During the first rush of optimism after the war, the municipal authorities decided to raze the old quarter and remove all the wooden houses in Straen, Skagen, Østervåg, Arneageren, and Holmen, leaving plenty of room for a spanking new industrial centre constructed of concrete and glass.

Modernity, particularly in architecture, was, it was generally agreed, the royal road to progress. When the local director of historic monuments, Einar Hedén, proposed a plan for restoring 33 houses in the old district of Straen in 1951, it therefore met with a very lukewarm reception. However, the economy being in a decline, the planned destruction was not put into effect either, and by 1956 many people had begun to have misgivings. As a result, Hedén's plan was adopted by the municipal council with a majority of one vote. The association for the preservation of "Old Stavanger" was founded in 1957, with Edén as its chairman.

In 1975 Old Stavanger was chosen as one of three pilot projects for conservation during the Year of the Environment. The old town, which now consisted of 160 houses, was to represent the coastal domestic architecture of Norway, with its low, white-painted, wood-panelled houses.

For a long period of its history, the herring fisheries and shipping were the backbone of Sta-

vanger's economy, but when the shoals of herring failed to appear and the sailing ships were replaced by steam, a new activity, the canning industry, gradually took over. The pioneer of this movement was a young man named Christian Bjelland, from Jæren, outside Stavanger. He began his career by selling brooms and rags and bones, and moved on to buying combs, rings, and brooches from the shops and selling them to farmers on market day. Gradually he built up his fortune, until in 1890 he was able to start a business canning sardines. Soon there was a world market for "Norwegian sardines". In periods Stavanger had up to 400 canning factories, most of whose production was exported. Even in the 1950s there were 50 canning factories in full operation, but not one remains today. Offshore petroleum has taken their place as Stavanger's new growth industry.

The Canning Museum in Old Stavanger is the only one of its kind in the world. The premises of Chr. Bjelland & Co. have been restored to the condition they were in when the firm was in its heyday, from 1890 to 1930, and turned into a museum. Among the exhibits is a display of the imaginative and colourful labels used for the sardine tins, which have become collector's items. There are 20,000 different labels altogether.

Throughout the nineteenth century, when herring fishing brought prosperity to the town for the first time in its history, Strandkaien was a busy and lively wharf, bordered by the traditional wharfhouses. Originally there were 172 of them, but most have been pulled down or turned into sardine factories. Behind the wharfhouses were the houses of the merchants, combining shops, offices, and living accommodation.

Two of the merchants' houses have been completely restored, and here we find the Maritime Museum. The maritime section shows the historical development of shipping and shipbuilding, and the rise of the port of Stavanger up to the present day, including the development of the petroleum industry. The museum contains a reconstruction of a sailmaker's workshop and shipping offices from the 1930s as well as a restored wharfhouse. The museum also has two boats, the *Anna af Sand* and the pleasure yacht *Wyern*, built by the renowned Colin Archer. The commercial section of the museum contains a clothing and food store from the turn of the century, the apartment of a merchant, and a memorial chamber dedicated to the Norwegian-Danish philosopher and geologist Henrich Steffens [1773–1845], who was born in this house, and who became known for being mainly responsible for introducing the romantic movement into Norway.

The oldest building in Old Stavanger is the Blidensol house in Gamle Strandgate, the main house belonging to the farm that originally owned much of the land around there. The history of the house can be traced back to 1767, but it was probably built at the beginning of the

eighteenth century. In recent years the Rosenkilde house and its surroundings have also been restored, opening up this part of town to the Market Square and Vågen.

Old Stavanger is today an attractive and lively part of town. All the houses are lived in or turned into shops, workshops for arts and crafts, and even a smithy. Almost 200 white-painted houses, with carved window frames and colourful front doors, usually opening directly onto the narrow, winding streets, create a charming old-fashioned small-town atmosphere, with gas lighting, tiny unexpected squares, and a profusion of flowers.

STAVANGER CATHEDRAL

"The heart of man never changes." The truth of the novelist Sigrid Undset's words was shown by an event that took place in 1128, but which could just as easily have occurred today. If it had, the newspaper headlines would have run something like this: "Bishop refuses to wed divorced king", or "Royal bridegroom bribes bishop".

The king in question was Sigurd Jorsalfar, and in 1128 he was on his way to Stavanger to persuade the bishop to perform an act that would undoubtedly contravene the rules of the church. The king had divorced his lawful wife Malmfrid, a princess of Novgorod, and wished to marry a woman named Cecilia. The bishop of Bergen had refused to give the couple his blessing, and the king was hoping that Bishop Reinald, from Winchester in England, would oblige.

The king arrived at a good time. Like many other building projects, Stavanger Cathedral was eating money, and Bishop Reinald saw this as a good opportunity to strike a bargain; he agreed to marry the king in exchange for a large donation to the cathedral. King Sigurd had in other respects been a benefactor to the church; he had introduced the payment of tithes in kind, which the bishop was able to sell or exchange for other goods.

Now the walls of the Anglo-Norman, or romanesque, basilica

could continue to rise on the height between Bredevannet and the harbour. It was dedicated to the English saint St. Swithin, whose arm was the most prized relic in the church's possession. The

town of Stavanger grew up around the church and the bishopric, which was established at the same time; until the beginning of the twelfth century there had been nothing more than a collection of houses at the inner end of Vågen. In *A Cicerone of Stavanger*, published in 1868, we read that, "Recording the history of the Cathedral is almost the same as recording that of Stavanger itself; St. Swithin's Town stands or falls with its church."

In 1272 "the red cock crowed" in Stavanger, and not even the church was spared by the flames. It is possible, though, that at the time the fire was regarded as providential by the churchmen. For their numbers were expanding, and during the 1200s it was not unusual to rebuild or expand a chancel to make more room. Thus what remained of the romanesque chancel was pulled down and a new chancel, which took up over two-thirds of the entire nave of the church, was built in the latest style of ecclesiastical architecture – the gothic. All the elements are here: high arching cross-vaults, slender pointed windows, and elegantly carved capitals ornamented with leaves and flowers. To the east the chancel ends in a high gable flanked by two towers and featuring a large quartered window topped by three rose windows – a superb example of Norwegian gothic.

After the Norwegian Reformation in 1536 all St. Swithin's protection was not enough to prevent the Danish king's depredations, which removed everything, even the saint's arm. Even the church bells were sent to Copenhagen to be smelted down. Fate caught up with them, however, for the ship carrying them went down near Håstein off the Jæren coast, and here their remains are still said to lie.

During the seventeenth century, however, a renewed interest in the church was evinced by the citizens. Local civic and church dignitaries donated gifts, "for the ornamentation of the church and in commemoration of themselves". It was during this period that the baroque decorations were added to the interior. A Scot named Andrew [Anders] Smith, who had settled in Nor-

way, was responsible for this. His pulpit, dated 1658, is a masterpiece of baroque art. Smith's career, which lasted from 1658 to 1694, was a busy one, and he seems to have been responsible for much of the church's decoration during this period, from the magnificent frames around the memorial tablets to, perhaps, the portraits. The latter is not certain; it is also possible that they were painted by Peter Bilthugger, one of Smith's contemporaries.

No other Norwegian church has retained so much of its baroque interior as Stavanger Cathedral. This is in spite of the fact that in the last century public opinion was in favour of remov-

ing all traces of the "later additions that harmonized so poorly with the church". In 1867–70 the architect Conrad Fredrik von der Lippe undertook a fairly sweeping restoration, in neo-gothic, which posed a considerable threat to Smith's masterpieces. Fortunately the most important of these were preserved, and a later restoration, in 1938–42, under the direction of the architect Gerhard Fischer, did its best to restore the romanesque and gothic elements of the Middle Ages. Among the twentieth-century artists whose works are to be found in the cathedral are Emmanuel Vigeland, Stinius Fredriksen, Frida Hansen, and Victor Sparre.

$\mathcal{U}$TSTEIN ABBEY

Snorre's Saga tells of the Battle of Hafrsfjord in 872, when "the great king of the Eastmen, he who lives at Utstein" put his enemies to flight. The king was Harald Fairhair and the battle was one of the many he waged against the lesser kings Kjotve [the Fat] and Haklang [the Long-Chinned] in his attempt to unify Norway under one king. Harald spent many periods of his life at Utstein, although the Norwegian kings at this time moved about the country and had no permanent residence.

This tiny group of islands in Boknafjord was an attractive settlement long before Harald Fairhair's time; there are traces of habitation right back to 7500–8000 BC. There were fish in the sea, good grazing land and fertile farmland, and furthermore the island of Klosterøy, where the king established his residence, was sheltered and had a good harbour, and commanded a strategic position at the entrance to the fjords leading to Stavanger and the Ryfylke fjords further inland.

There are few traces of King Harald's residence today; the ruins of the abbey date from around 1260, from the reign of King Magnus Lagabøte. In 1264 the king moved to Bergen on the death of his father, King Haakon Haakonsson, and donated Utstein to the Augustine monks of the monastery of St. Olav in Stavanger. The abbey at Utstein was dedicated to St. Laurentius and was part of the diocese of Stavanger.

The buildings, in the English gothic style, reflect the wealth of the abbey. It owned no less than 150 properties scattered about the county of Rogaland and Sunnhordland district, which supplied the abbey with grain, butter, meat, fish, and other products. The surplus was so large that the monks were able to run a thriving export business, and had their own cargo boat on a regular run to England, where much of their trade was conducted.

The calm of the monastic life, with its regular intervals of work and prayer, was relieved every now and then by an occasional scandal, especially conflicts with the Bishop of Stavanger. In 1333 Abbot Eirik of Utstein was accused by Bishop Erik Ogmundssøn of decadence. Abbot Eirik then sued the bishop, who in his absence had taken possession of the abbey by force. The case went all the way up to the Pope, who may have taken the abbot's part; at any rate in 1341 the bishop of Bergen wrote a letter to Bishop Erik recommending him to make his peace with the abbot of Utstein without prejudicing the reputation or interests of either party.

Two hundred years later, in 1510, the abbey's fortunes seem to have reached a low ebb, and the abbot, Truls or Trofwels, was forced to sell a plot of land "for reasons of necessity and because of the decline in fortunes and great poverty of the abbey". His successor, Abbot Henrik Benediktsson, ignored both the abbey's obligation to pay taxes and tithes and the bishop's visiting rights. Once again, the Bishop of Stavanger occupied the abbey by force of arms, terrorizing the abbot and monks and seizing goods and food. The abbot was imprisoned in the tower of the Bishop's Palace in Stavanger, but managed to escape and write to the King: "... but then by the grace of God, the Blessed Virgin Mary and St. Anne, I was able to escape into the wilderness and live off grass and water."

With the Reformation, Utstein became crown property, and remained so until 1665. In 1700 it was taken over by the Garmann family, and under Christopher Garmann it entered a period of

prosperity. Garmann was strongly influenced by the ideas of the enlightenment, and he restored the church and buildings of Utstein, improved sheep-breeding in the district round about [his pamphlet entitled *Thoughts on Fine-wooled Sheep and on Methods of Improving Coarse Wool* makes interesting reading], founded a scholarly society, Det Nyttige Selskab, in Bergen, and took an active and inspiring part in the cultural life of Bergen.

He was also responsible for Utstein's ghost. His second wife, Cecilie Catharina Widding, had made him promise on her deathbed never to take another wife, a promise he kept for 20 years before breaking. On the eve of his wedding to a new wife on 9 February 1779, Cecilie Catharina appeared to him, and he died eight days later. Cecilie Catharina still haunts the abbey, in the form of a lady in white.

In 1885 Utstein became the property of the Schanke family, and in 1926 the abbey buildings and the farm were separated. The buildings were restored during the 1950s and are now used for conferences and seminars.

ÆGATUNET

The mountain rose, black and threatening, 1550 metres above the sea. But before it lay the fjord, open and welcoming. In the summer the land was green and fertile, and people saw that the mountain gave protection, and they built their houses in its lee. But the mountain was steep and dangerous, and many lives were lost. Finally, however, people found a place where the avalanches did not reach, a sloping shelf below a craggy outcrop called Tveiteberget. The mountain divided the river into two at this point, and snow or rocks rushing down the mountainside were diverted. The avalanches continued to destroy the occasional crop, but at least the houses were safe, and the people of Agatunet no longer feared for their lives. [The name Aga may come from the word *age*, meaning fear.]

Nowadays large numbers of visitors stop at Agatunet in Ullensvang in Hardanger, for the road runs just below this very unusual hamlet, which is now owned by a trust and has been listed for protection since 1938.

The way farms and farm buildings are grouped together around a *tun* [a barton, or farmyard] shows interesting regional variations

throughout Norway, and Agatunet is characteristic of western Norway, where the position of the buildings was influenced by the local system of land division. Originally Aga was a single large farm, which was divided into two, the upper and lower bartons, and later into a number of separate farms. For practical reasons, however, the houses were clustered together in the centre of the farmland. Every time the farms were divided, more houses were built within the central cluster, and more land was cultivated on the outskirts of the property. The system meant that after a while what had been a single farm began to resemble eighteenth-century Germany, with an innumerable number of small states. Each farm had its own main house, stables, barn, storehouses, and so on. On the outskirts of the barton was the smithy and a shed for drying grain, meat, fish, and so on, beside the stream was a mill, and down by the edge of the fjord were the boathouses and fishing sheds.

Many of the individual buildings in Agatunet have changed over the years. The oldest house is the Lagmannsstova, or Judge's House, and was

built by Sigurd Brynjolfsson, judge in the Court of the Gulating and a trusted counsellor of King Eirik Magnusson. His grave can still be seen in Ullensvang Church. The 7 by 7.5 metre building rests on a stone basement one full storey high, a very unusual feature in the countryside, although it was common enough in medieval towns. The barton also had its own chapel, almost 16 metres long, but this was pulled down in 1811, and now all that is left of it is a small bronze gothic bell hanging in the Judge's House.

Before road no. 555 ran past Aga, there were no roads other than those in the barton itself. As the number of farm buildings grew, it became more and more difficult to thread one's way between the houses, so finally cobbled streets were laid, the main street separating the upper from the lower barton.

The number of farms and inhabitants at Aga have varied considerably over the centuries. We know that in 1871 there were a total of 159 people on the farms, and that all the families were yeomen farmers; in other words, they all owned their land. When the trust was founded in 1938 there were nine farms at Aga, all owned by descendants of Sigurd Brynjolfsson. It is not surprising that the local families have always had a strong sense of lineage, as the following story illustrates. It was written down by the Danish-Norwegian philosopher Henrich Steffens.

On his way to Aga one day, Steffens fell in with a Danish colonel and the two of them went together. Arriving at Aga, they went to one of the farmhouses and asked whether the farmer's wife could give them some dinner. "And don't worry if everything's a little dirty," said the colonel, "We're used to roughing it." The farmer's wife said nothing.

The two men went for a walk while the meal was being prepared, and when they came back they were welcomed by the farmer himself, an imposing man with a great grey beard, dressed in a handsome white frieze jacket. The table was laid with a white cloth and silver cutlery, and a row of wine bottles stood ready on a side table. The first course was a soup that the colonel found quite delicious. When his hostess entered the room bearing a covered dish, the colonel licked his lips in anticipation and said that this was sure to be something good. "Well," replied the woman, "I don't know I'm sure. We don't eat it ourselves, but since you asked for it, you may have it." And she took off the lid, showing a dish filled to the brim with dirt.

The end of the story is also characteristic. For the rest of the meal maintained the same high standard as the soup, and at the end of it the colonel, against Steffens' advice, offered to pay, not wishing to be in the debt of a mere farmer. The farmer was indignant. "Do you think I can't afford to give a little food to a poor Dane," he inquired with scorn, "without having to be paid like an innkeeper?"

THE BARONY OF ROSENDAL

In Rosendal [which means "the valley of roses"], "one of the most beautiful hamlets in Hardanger", lies a simple building in early baroque, surrounded by a formal garden; behind it towers the 889 metre-high crag of Mamangerknuten. This is the barony of Rosendal, the only one of its kind in Norway, which was built in 1663–65 by a Danish nobleman named Ludvig Rosenkrantz, who was employed in the Norwegian army.

The marriage of the 30-year-old Rosenkrantz to the well-born Karen Mowatt in 1658 marked the end of all his money worries. His powerful and wealthy father-in-law, Axel Mowatt, gave him the farm of Hattegården and enabled him to pay off his debts, which he is said to have revealed as being 20,000 riksdaler "and a little over". His marriage also advanced his career; he progressed to commissary for the northern part of Norway, then rose to commissary general, governor of the shire [*amtmann*], and finally diocesan governor [*stiftamtmann*] in Stavanger.

With the death of his father-in-law in 1661, Ludvig Rosenkrantz became one of Norway's wealthiest men. In 1678 the estate became a barony, and the new baron was able to carve his coat of arms over the main gate, along with the

bold motto *Melius est mori in libertate quam vivere in servitute* ["Better to die free than live in servitude"]. A motto that must have been taken to heart by the cotters and leaseholders on the estate when Ludvig's youngest son, Axel, inherited the property, and they found out what it really meant to live in servitude. The finances of the estate were in a bad way, and the cost of keeping up the barony weighed heavily on the budget. However, by milking the farmers of all they were worth, Axel Rosenkrantz managed to rid himself of his debts. The young baron had a club foot, and his nickname, "Baron Klump", cannot have made him feel more kindly towards the world. His deformity was probably one of the reasons for his "gross and drunken" behaviour, which caused his death; in 1723 he fell down in a drunken stupor and killed himself. Although his epitaph says that Rosendal was "bathed in tears" at his death, this seems unlikely.

A bad reputation was not all Axel Rosenkrantz left behind him, however. The estate's debts had been paid, and the property had been increased; improvements had been made to the main house at Rosendal and the church at Kvinnherad had been renovated. He was also responsible for much of the layout of the well-designed garden, and is said to have spent a good deal of time in the little summer house in the south-west corner, so much so that it developed "a notorious reputation".

After Rosenkrantz' death the estate became the property of the crown and changed owners several times. In 1749, however, Edvard Londemann, Baron Rosencrone, made the property his family seat, and it remained in their possession until 1927. The Rosencrones were more conscious than their predecessors that "noblesse oblige", and the last baron's eldest son, Marcus Gerhard Hoff Rosencrone, ran Rosendal as a model farm. He had also inherited his father's literary interests and his love of music, was a friend of the composer Halfdan Kjerulf, corresponded with the writer Bjørnstjerne Bjørnson and with Asbjørnsen and Moe, the great collectors of Norwegian folk tales, and in general was a gifted and enlightened man. King Carl XV of Sweden and Norway asked him to join his government, and offered him the post of minister in Paris. But "the Baron" as he was always called, in spite of the fact that titles had been abolished, refused all offers. He preferred to devote himself to his beloved Rosendal and to the local community. Popular education was one of his great interests, and he supported the local school and was a keen follower of the ideas of the Danish preacher and poet Grundtvig, who established popular high schools.

The de Hoff-Rosencrone family held the estate until 1900, when passed to a collateral branch of the family, the Weises. On the death of the last Weis-Rosencrone, in 1927, the property was left to the University of Oslo. Today it is run by a trust and is open to the public.

"The building is a square box in two stories, with a courtyard in the middle. It has neither style nor beauty, but if you go inside, the house is worth a visit," wrote a local writer, Jens Tvedt, at the turn of the century. The house is worth a visit now too, not only to see the rooms, but also to attend the various events arranged by the trust, like concerts, art exhibitions, demonstrations of carding and spinning or traditional baking and the *Baroni Spelet*, a play about the early history of the barony.

THE GLACIERS

*"There's a land lying close to perpetual snow,
Where life only blooms in the crannies below"*

In a few words, the national poet Bjørnson has expressed the essence of the dramatic contrasts in the Norwegian landscape, which for hundreds of years have caused visitors to marvel at the splendour of the scenery, and which have so strongly influenced the Norwegian character and way of thinking.

And it was the action of the glaciers that formed these contrasts, these steep mountains and narrow valleys. The mass of snow and ice

that forms a glacier is in constant movement, starting high up on the mountain plateaus and moving slowly and inexorably down the valleys or spreading outwards to form ice sheets. Glaciers are formed when the snowfall is so great

that the melting and drainage during the spring and summer do not carry all the new snow away. This snow remains and is packed down by the next year's fall, and with the addition of melted snow running into it, it crystallizes into ice. The pressure of new masses of snow accumulating on top of the ice causes it to move outwards and downwards, altering the landscape as it goes.

Thus the size and number of glaciers depends on the climate, and Norway has one of the largest areas of glaciers in Europe. Much of it is left over from the ice cap that once covered the country. Although the last ice age was succeeded by a warmer period, about 2500 years ago the weather became colder and the glaciers expanded. Some of them have continued growing well into the present century, but most of the Norwegian glaciers have been shrinking since the middle of the eighteenth century.

Today about 4600 square kilometres of mainland Norway are covered by glaciers. The largest of them, Jostedalsbreen in Sogn, is a typical plateau glacier, from which 28 different tongues run down into the surrounding valleys. One of these is Briksdalsbreen near the lake of Oldevatnet, which attracts more visitors than any other glacier in Norway. For many tourists this region, with its high jagged mountains, eternal ice, its deep valleys and fjords, represents the very essence of Norway. In this part of the country the glaciers are fairly accessible, since Briksdalsbreen can be reached without too much physical effort, by horse and carriage.

The Black Ice? Can ice be black? This is the name of the next largest glacier in Norway, which covers a large area of Salten, in Nordland county. The name comes from the deep blue of the ice, which forms a startling contrast to the white of the surrounding snow. It is the lowest-lying of the glaciers, with its lowest point only 20 metres above sea level, and can be admired both from the sea and from the road. The Black Ice was regarded in north Norwegian legend as the work of supernatural agencies, and there are several stories about how this vast ice mass came

into being.

The third largest glacier, Folgefonni in Hordaland, is also surrounded by legend and myth. The story, which has more than a suggestion of Noah's Ark about it, goes that where the great glacier now lies there used to be a fertile valley called Folgedalen, with seven parishes. But the people of Folgedalen were so proud and ungodly that the Lord decided to punish them by sending a storm of sleet and snow, which went on for 10 weeks without stopping. The whole valley was filled with snow, and all living things perished. Although this is only a legend, it is known that the ice cap continued to expand in Norway until the beginning of the 1700s, and that the movements of the glaciers did destroy many farms. The legend may therefore have had its roots in a natural disaster. Moreover the location of Folgefonni is unique; unlike the other glaciers in Norway, it lies very close to both the fjord and the forest.

The Norwegian Mountain Touring Association has been arranging courses for many years in hiking over glaciers and climbing on ice. Glacier skiing has also become popular, and in the spring, when the snow has melted in other parts of Norway, the glaciers can become quite crowded.

For those who would like to find out about glaciers without actually walking on them, the Norwegian Glacier Museum opened its doors to the public in 1991. After entering this imaginative building, designed by Sverre Fehn, through a portal resembling a cleft in a glacier, one meets a creaking, cracking, sliding imitation of a real glacier in the deep blue half darkness within. Models and interactive exhibits demonstrate how the ice forms and alters the landscape. There is a cinema showing a simulated flight and a climbing trip over Jostedalsbreen, which, with its frozen wastes, dizzy heights, and narrow gorges, is an experience not likely to be forgotten.

The Glacier Museum, which is situated in Fjærland, Sogn, is more than a museum; it arranges activities and courses for adults and children and is a centre for research as well.

THE FALLS OF VØRINGSFOSSEN

A river runs down from Tindhølen, on the Hardanger plateau, 1213 metres above sea level. It runs north-west, gathering speed and taking with it the rivers Leiro and Isdøla, from the Hardangerjøkulen glacier, purls along the broad flat valley of Bjoreidalen to Fossli, then picks up speed and hurls itself straight off the cliff, falling 182 metres down into Måbødalen.

This enormous mass of water is known as Vøringsfossen, and is one of the most magnificent falls in a country plentifully endowed with waterfalls. For thousands of years it thundered down from its height, but it was not until the beginning of the last century, with the dawning awareness of natural beauties that came with the romantic period, that people became conscious of Vøringsfossen as a natural phenomenon. Professor Christopher Hansteen visited the falls in 1821 and was deeply impressed; it was he who opened the eyes of the general public to their splendour. Within a year the artist Johannes Flintoe was there with his easel and brush, and he was followed by a number of the more nature-loving citizens of Christiania, who combined it with a visit to Geilo, Ustevatnet and Sysendalen, which were also becoming known for their magnificent scenery.

It has been said that the local farmers must have received the news of the "discovery" of Vøringsfossen in the same spirit as the Indians greeted Columbus' discovery of America – with bemusement. To them the falls were probably simply a part of their natural surroundings, which had always been there. It must have been astonishing to witness the oohs and aahs of amazement with which strangers greeted this well-known feature of their landscape.

Vøringsfossen was not the only such discovery to be made during the last century. An article written at the turn of the century points out that "The discovery of [the mountains of] Jotunheimen, [the falls of] Rjukanfossen, and Vøringsfossen were the events that really paved the way for the introduction of tourism in Norway". The improvement in roads and communications and the increase in wealth that came in the train of industrialization helped to strengthen the ideas of the romantic movement, through which the natural beauties of landscapes were beginning to be appreciated. Wild, uncultivated country, that had hitherto been regarded as sinister and quite bereft of any usefulness or beauty, was suddenly perceived as expressing grandeur and nobility. In Norway the romantic movement had a strongly nationalistic aspect because of the country's dawning independence, and painters flocked to immortalize the romantic landscapes and mighty mountains of their country, the most zealous being Flintoe, closely followed by Hans Gude, Adolph Tidemand, and J. C. Dahl. It was during this period of increased travelling for pleasure that, in 1868, the Norwegian Mountain Touring Association was founded.

The writer Jens Tvedt visited the falls during the 1870s. The road had been newly laid by the Mountain Touring Association, but it must have been steep and poorly surfaced, for he wrote of it that "they have not been able to afford to make it any better". The falls, however, rendered him speechless: "What power! Such sublime grandeur that I have no words to describe i."

Tvedt saw the falls from above, from the site occupied by the Fossli Hotel today. This provides the best and most dramatic view of the falls and of the rainbow formed by the boiling clouds of spray. The name *Vøring* probably means either the "steam" from the falls or that which is held in *vørdnad*, respect. There is a third possibility, which is accounted for in the following legend.

One winter's night a long, long time ago, a man named Vøring was travelling on skis across Hardangervidda on his way to Eidfjord. It was dark, and snowing so thickly that he could barely see his hand in front of his face. After a while he became conscious of an approaching sound like far-away thunder, and he wondered whether to stop and see what it was. But the snow was so thick, and the night so cold, that he did not dare turn aside, so he continued on his way. And suddenly he found himself on the edge of a precipice; a bottomless black abyss opened in front of him, filled with a deafening roar. He tried to throw himself to one side, but it was too late; down he fell, hundreds of feet, and disappeared into the cauldron of foam at the bottom. Not even his body was found, but the people of the valley called the falls after him.

In 1980 the falls were harnessed to provide hydroelectric power.

ℳ ØLSTERTUNET

Arnfinn and Botolv, of Mølstertunet in the village of Voss, each had their own farm. But although each farm had its own main house and stables, barn, bakehouse, storehouses, and smithy, they were all built close together around the same barton, or *tun*, 16 buildings in all, housing 27 people. Here the two families could help and support each other, rejoicing together in good times and, it is to be hoped, comforting each other in bad.

This system of more than one family sharing a common barton goes back a long way and one assumes that it had proved satisfactory here at Mølstertunet. For when Arnfinn and Botolv gave up farming in 1927, and the two farms were made over to the Voss Folk Museum, they had been in existence for a good 400 years and perhaps longer.

Mølstertunet lies on a south-facing hillside above the village of Voss, in Hordaland county.

The first settlement in this area probably dates back to pre-Viking times, but the oldest written source that cites Mølster is dated 1387.

Mølstertunet was not among the largest or finest of the bartons in Voss. When the director general of the Central Office of Historic Monuments, Harry Fett, visited Mølstertunet in 1918, he wrote: "Coming to Mølster is like going back into the past, like meeting our forefathers." What distinguished it from the others, and made it historically unique, was the fact that the buildings all stood exactly as they were first built, with nothing moved or added to. The Norwegian building style, with its small, specialized buildings constructed of notched logs, made it relatively easy to

move houses about, and the fact that this has not been done is what makes Mølstertunet so unusual. In other words, the barton provides a completely authentic picture of a living and working environment as it has evolved gradually and naturally over the centuries.

The main houses, Arnfinn's House and Botolv's House, both date from the 1850s; otherwise most of the others were built towards the end of the seventeenth and beginning of the eighteenth centuries, and up to about the 1870s. The oldest building is probably sixteenth century, and when it was first built it was the main farmhouse; later it was used for baking, brewing and preparing the slaughtered carcases of meat for the table.

Mølstertunet now has its own museum, containing a collection of arts and crafts, furniture, tools, and other exhibits illustrating the cultural history of the area.

Finnesloftet in Voss, which dates back to about 1250, was probably a drinking hall and is the oldest non-ecclesiastical wooden building in Norway. In the old days, in the Middle Ages and the time of the Vikings, drinking bouts were a well-established custom, with roots reaching right back to heathen times, when sacrificial feast were held where toasts were drunk in memory of the ancestors. When Olav Tryggvason introduced Christianity he allowed these drinking bouts, with their religious connotations, to be incorporated into the Christian rituals, and even had them established by law. Thus at the great church festivals, Christmas, Easter, the midsummer feast of St. Hans, and Michaelmas, ceremonial drinking bouts were held. Similar to these were the *drikkegilde*, where everyone paid for or brought their own drink. Snorre's saga about Olav Kyrre tells how the king introduced the idea of such *drikkegilde* from abroad, where they were part of the Christian ceremonial. Special places were set aside for holding these feasts, especially, says the saga, in towns and marketplaces, where they replaced the old custom of alternating between different hosts. These new *drikkegilde* were usually dedicated to a saint, and special drinking halls were built to accommodate them.

Finne Farm was a manor farm in the Middle Ages, and the owner probably built the hall for his own festivities, but on the major feast days, such as Michaelmas, on 29 September, which was an important saint's day connected with the harvest, he would almost certainly have opened it up and allowed a great public feast to be held.

Finnesloftet has three floors. The drink was stored on the ground floor, dancing was held for the young people on the first floor, and above that was a room where the better type of guest and the older people could sit and talk. The building is now owned by the Society for the Preservation of Norwegian Ancient Monuments.

HE FLÅM RAILWAY

It was a winter's night in 1884, and it was already getting dark when the young man realized that he had lost his way. The path he had been following had disappeared, and he found himself on the edge of a precipice: "I stood before a gorge many hundred feet deep, and looked down into the abyss of a narrow valley – Flåmsdalen." The man who described his frightening experience in these words was none other than the explorer Fridtjof Nansen, in training for one of his many expeditions.

The mountains rise 1300–1700 metres on both sides of the 20 kilometre-long valley of Flåmsdal, which runs from the end of the Aurlandsfjord to Myrdal station on the railway line from Oslo to Bergen. But when Nansen so abruptly discovered Flåmsdalen there was neither a Bergen line nor a branch line to Flåm; a steep, winding pack road was the only means of communication with the outside world. The farms in the valley provided a poor living, and not a few of the inhabitants had emigrated to America. So that when the work on the Bergen

line began in 1894, and a transport road was built through the valley, this provided a much-needed opportunity for work for many of the inhabitants.

But the new railway line was to run above the valley, 867 metres up, to be precise, and would not provide any link between the valley and the rest of the world. When the idea of the Bergen railway was first mooted, during the 1890s, there had been a proposal to build a branch line linking Myrdal with the Aurlandsfjord, but the people of Flåmsdalen had to wait until 1908 before a parliamentary decision was finally made confirming this.

The people of Bergen had held a torchlight procession to celebrate the decision to build the Bergen railway in 1894; the people of Flåmsdalen showed their delight in their own particular way. The station master at Myrdal station and his staff solemnly raised the flag in thanks and had themselves photographed standing around the flagstaff.

Once the decision was made, however, there seemed to be no hurry to implement it, and no work at all was done on the proposed railway until 1923, and then it took 20 years to complete the work. There were endless difficulties. The line was short but the terrain was extremely difficult and made great demands on the skill of the engineers. To complicate the process the funds granted for the work fluctuated a good deal, especially in the poor economic climate at the end of the 1920s. During this period the work force, which was never more than 260 men, was down to 70–80. When the line was finally opened on 1 August 1940, the country was at war and no real celebration was possible.

Even today, the Flåm railway stands out as a masterpiece of technology, without any parallel in the other Nordic countries. The 20 kilometre long electric railway line has a normal gauge, with a maximum axle load for rolling stock of 18 tons. In order to cope with the steep gradient – the line rises 864 metres in the course of its short length – the upper part is laid out in a series of hairpin bends, much of it inside the mountain. Thus it zig-zags down the mountainside, appearing and reappearing from 20 tunnels, which

make up 28 per cent of its length. The journey takes just an hour, and provides glimpses of one breathtaking view after another. Among the most imposing are Kjosfossen, which is one of Norway's most photographed waterfalls, and Rjoandefossen, which hurls itself 140 metres off the cliff edge down into the valley.

But what really impresses the visitor, even more than the engineering skills and the magnificent scenery, is the work of the railwaymen, or *rallare*, as they were popularly called. Two of the tunnels were drilled by machinery, but all the rest was manual work. Hand drills, sledge-hammers, dynamite and their own muscles were the only tools they had. Most of the work was done as piecework, which worked out at an hourly rate of about two crowns an hour; when paid by the day they received a little over one crown an hour. But the *rallare* were a hardy race. After a day of backbreaking work on the railway, they were always ready for a hunting or fishing expedition or some form of sport. Sports clubs were formed, ski jumps were built, competitions were held. And it is said that the whole valley used to look forward to Saturday nights, when dances were held in the workmen's huts.

URNES STAVE CHURCH

In the twilight of the spring evening, the bells of Urnes Stave Church are ringing the faithful to Vespers. About 20 to 30 kilometres out near the mouth of the fjord, King Sverre and his men, known as *birkebeinerne,* or birch-legs, because of their habit of using birch-bark as leggings, are fighting King Magnus Erlingsson and his supporters in the civil war that raged between north and west Norway and east and south Norway from 1174 to 1217. The day is St. Vitus' Mass, and the year is 1184. The rumours of war have certainly reached the people of Urnes, and they are probably praying for the victory of King

Magnus, for here at Urnes many of the families have at least one member among this king's supporters. But their prayers were in vain, and the victory went to King Sverre, who thereby gained control over much of the country south of Trondheim.

The stave church at Urnes has been called the queen of stave churches, standing as it does on a rise about 120 metres above sea level, with magnificent views inland to Luster and out over the panorama of the Sognefjord. People have been gathering here to pray to the White Christ for peace, for victory, or for good harvests since the time of the Vikings. Urnes Stave Church is probably the oldest in the country, and parts of it actually come from an even older church. Archaeological excavations made in 1956–57 showed traces of another, tiny church, with its wall-posts planted in holes in the ground. The oldest decorated parts of the building are from this earlier church, and perhaps from an even older one. The main entrance and two gables are among the oldest structural elements. The decorations are unique to this particular church, and have been christened the Urnes style.

The Urnes style has been called the swan song of the heathen style of animal ornamentation, but similar motifs have also been found on a number of Swedish runic stones in Uppland county, which date back to about 1060, by which time even the most obscure corners of Sweden and Norway had been converted to Christianity. However, the Urnes carvings are completely uninfluenced by the early Christian style, which was the romanesque style that was being adopted in other parts of the country, such as Ringerike. In the latter style tendrils and plant ornamentation was supplanting the animal motif. The characteristic four-footed animals of the Urnes style, and the graceful interplay of intertwining bands of animals of different widths, were obviously carved by a great artist. The style was so vigorous that traces of it can be found far into the gothic era.

The interior of Urnes Stave Church is marked by the post-Reformation, with its closed, carved pews, gallery, and choir screen all dating back to the seventeenth century, and its pulpit and altarpiece dated 1695 and 1699 respectively. The medieval proportions of the interior are, however, unchanged. The elaborate form of the nave is especially interesting, with its pillars or "staves" with their richly carved capitals. An ear-

ly medieval Calvary group above the rood arch shows Christ in the typical fashion of the time: as a triumphal king with a crown on his head. The iron Viking-ship candlestick on the altar is supposed to be one of the oldest candlesticks in existence. The altar also bears a pair of very rare and beautiful enamelled metal candlesticks from Limoges, in France, dating from the thirteenth century. It is tempting to wonder how on earth these sophisticated objects found their way to this tiny out-of-the-way Norwegian hamlet.

Urnes Stave Church has attracted many legends, among them the story of Habor, or Hagbard, and Signe, two unhappy lovers who shared many characteristics with Tristan and Isolde. The legend goes that the tragic love story took place at Urnes, and in olden days people were able to point out the site of the gallows where Habor was hanged, and the cage where Signe lived and where she killed herself out of grief. The church is also supposed to have contained a 100-foot long tapestry known as "Signe's tapestry". During fires, the tapestry was soaked in sea water and used to smother the flames.

There must have been a lot of fires in the village, since according to legend the tapestry got smaller and smaller through use. Finally pieces of Signe's tapestry are supposed to have been "from time immemorial cut off and given away as reliquaries".

ROLDHAUGEN

It was the 11 of June 1892, and over 5000 people were said to have arrived by train during the day. Every rock and tongue of land along the shore was black with people, and the waters of Nordåsvannet teemed with boats. The flames of bonfires flickered along the shore and on the islands dotted about the fjord. Every now and then the brilliant red or green of a firework briefly shot through the gathering darkness of the summer night. The sound of voices, laughter, and occasional cheers could be heard echoing over the glassy sea, with its mirrored reflection of the surrounding landscape.

Edvard and Nina Grieg were celebrating their silver wedding anniversary, the first celebration of any size to be held in their own home. It was attended by 100 invited guests; the rest were crowds from many miles around who had come to show their admiration for a great composer.

The Griegs had built Troldhaugen seven years previously, in 1885, as a refuge from the demands of a fame that was threatening to become overwhelming. For Grieg, unlike many composers, was famous in his own lifetime, and

his music was greeted with almost delirious adulation by the critics in Germany, England, Paris and Rome. On one concert tour, for example, when Edvard played and Nina sang, the whole of London

fell prey to "Grieg fever". And yet, although he had already written works like the Piano Concerto in A Minor, he wrote to his friend Frants Beyer, who had just finished building his own

house: "There is something inside me that cries out: A home! A home! Not until I have one will I be able to create something, and it is high time I began!" And so he, too, built a house near Beyer's, in the exquisite countryside near his birthplace, Bergen. For he longed for peace, and above all for contact with the Norwegian mountains and fjords, "home of wildness and mystery" as he called it. It was essential, he said, in order for him to "compose with his heart's blood".

There was little peace to be gained, however, even when the Griegs had settled in. For Grieg was his own worst enemy. He kept perpetual open house for all his friends, and on every concert tour overseas he issued lavish invitations to

visitors have to follow a path through an idyllic and rather overgrown little wood up to the villa. The rooms still exude the atmosphere of hospitality that they did in Grieg's day; on the peg in the hall hangs Grieg's old hat, and his battered suitcase still looks capable of making another journey.

For anyone who loves Grieg's music, a visit to the little red-painted cabin in the garden where he composed his Lyric Pieces and the song cycle *Haugtussa* brings him so close that we can almost hear Nina's warning words: "Edvard is working on his notes and is not to be disturbed."

And Grieg's notes are still an integral part of Troldhaugen. Weekly concerts are performed all through the summer, and every year during the Bergen International Music Festival concerts of Grieg's music are played on his own grand piano to an audience that fills the reception rooms, the conservatory and usually the garden as well. A new hall for chamber music called "Troldsalen", seating 200 people, was opened in 1985, and beneath the house the cellars have been transformed into a modern auditorium equipped for music research.

At the foot of a steep, westward-facing cliff, surrounded by ferns and rowan trees and silver birch, lies Grieg's tombstone, where he asked for his ashes to be laid. After laying the urn in place, Beyer wrote to Nina: "... And the sun has just gone down behind gold-rimmed clouds, and cast its last rays across the water to shine on Edvard's name. ... May his ashes rest in peace!"

come and visit him and discover "this fantastic and wonderful country, of which my art is such a poor reflection". And they came. The Beyers, who lived just across the water, used to hang sheets and light candles in the windows to tell the Griegs that yet another boatload of visitors was on its way. In a letter to Beyer dated 2 September 1902, Grieg wrote: "Today is the first day that Nina and I are alone at Troldhaugen."

Nor is it easy to be alone at Troldhaugen today. Since 1928, when it was officially opened to the public, the stream of visitors has steadily increased. And yet we still feel we are visiting a home rather than a museum. Buses and cars have to park some way from the house, and

THE FORTRESS OF BERGENHUS

In 1261 a great feast was held in Bergen – King Magnus, later known as Magnus Lagabøte, was celebrating both his wedding to the Danish princess Ingeborg and his coronation, and the feasting went on for three days. Two thousand guests

were entertained in the "Hall of Stone" and in two other halls, according to Haakon's saga. King Magnus' father, Haakon Haakonsson, had also celebrated his coronation at the same place, but in 1247 there was only a small stone church, and the guests had had to make do with a boathouse down by the shore. What is more, it had rained. It is said that this was the event that really impelled King Haakon to build the great stone hall of Håkonshallen.

This is not the beginning of the story, however. In about the year 1100 King Øystein Magnusson constructed a large royal hall of wood at the tip of the peninsula, and thus marked the official establishment of the royal residence in Bergen. Half a century later the imposing bulk of Christchurch stood close by, a visible symbol of Olav Kyrre's plan to make Bergen the permanent seat of the diocese of western Norway. In this way an ecclesiastical, worldly, and military centre of power was established at the entrance to Bergen harbour.

Haakon Haakonsson's building fever was unabated after building Håkonshallen; by the time he died in 1263 he had enlarged the royal residence by a number of stone buildings and a surrounding wall with two castellated gateways. His son Magnus took over, repairing Håkonshallen after a fire in 1266 and constructing a fortified tower, now known as the Rosenkrantz Tower, in 1270. By the beginning of the next century a complete medieval king's residence stood on the point.

Håkonshallen has always been, and still is, a splendid banqueting hall, an appropriate building for great occasions. However, during the union with Denmark, when the seat of royal power moved to Copenhagen, Håkonshallen fell into disuse as a residence, and was even used as a storehouse for a time. It stood neglected and ignored until the 1840s, when its history made an immediate appeal to the national romantic movement, and it was restored and later decorated by the artist Gerhard Munthe.

The Rosenkrantz Tower has had a colourful history and has been altered and rebuilt many times. In 1513 it was severely damaged by fire and during the 1530s the gunpowder chamber exploded and much of the tower collapsed. It continued to be patched up and repaired sporadically until 1562, when the governor of the castle, Erik Rosenkrantz, decided to renovate it and make it his official residence. Craftsmen were imported from Scotland to repair and fortify the tower, and in 1563, the date carved on the facade, it was completed and more or less in its present form.

When absolute monarchy was introduced in Denmark-Norway in 1660, civil and military authority were separated, and Bergenhus became a purely military fortress. It was soon to prove its use, for in 1665, at the Battle of Vågen, the first and only shots ever to be directed at an enemy were fired from the walls of the castle. Today Håkonshallen and the Rosenkrantz Tower are all that remains of Bergenhus Castle, and between them lies Slottsgården, surrounded by white-washed military barracks from the early 1700s.

In 1944 a disastrous explosion in Bergen har-bour caused part of the tower to collapse, and a fire broke out in Håkonshallen, but the damage was not too great to be repaired. A restored Håkonshallen was opened in 1961, 700 years to the day after the wedding that inaugurated it, and the Tower, which contains exhibitions of among other things military history, was re-opened to the public in 1966.

ST. MARY'S CHURCH, BERGEN

"When King Sverre came to the Church of St. Mary he met Jon Hallkjellsson. He prayed for mercy, and the king granted him mercy, him and his two sons, Ragnvald and Hallkjell." The description in Sverre's saga of King Sverre's attack on King Magnus Erlingsson and his men in 1183 is the first written source that mentions St. Mary's Church. At this time the church was fairly new; it is thought to have been built in about 1130–70. In the twelfth century Bergen had many churches: the Church of St. Olav, the Church of the Cross, the Church of St. Nicholas, the Stone Church, Christchurch, and many more. But the twin-towered romanesque Church of St. Mary, in the form of a basilica like the more southern cathedrals of Europe, was renowned for its beauty, as befitted a church dedicated to the Blessed Virgin. And for the seafarers who came sailing into the harbour, it was more than a landmark, it was a haven where they could seek to rid themselves of a heavy burden of sin.

The two towers are still clearly visible today to visitors approaching Bergen by sea, and although they form a less soaring contrast to their surroundings than they did in the Middle Ages, both they and the church still retain an impressive beauty. The church is the oldest building as well as the oldest parish church in Bergen. The main body is still the same as it was after its restoration from the fire that damaged it in 1248. It is also the only church in Norway, apart from Nidaros Cathedral in Trondheim, to have a triforium, a gallery of arches above the nave and below the clerestory windows. With its two west towers, its richly carved south entrance, and its nave and aisles, it occupies a special place in Norwegian medieval architecture. Its imposing dimensions indicate that it may have played a significant role among the churches of Bergen, perhaps as the main church for the town as a whole. We know that the citizens of the town held their Thing in the churchyard here, and that their banqueting hall was nearby.

For some time the church was known as the German Church because it was patronized by the German Hanseatic merchants and their descendants from 1408 to 1788. The last sermon in German was actually delivered there as late as 1868. It was also the German merchants who were responsible for many of the rich furnishings, which are clear indications of their flourishing trade. The oldest of these is the high gothic triptych, which is from north Germany, probably painted in Lübeck at the end of the fifteenth century. In the centre panel we find the Virgin and Child surrounded by St. Olav, St. Anthony, St. Catherine, and St. Dorothea. The Virgin is shown in the form of the woman in Revelations: "upon her head a crown of twelve stars". The two side panels show the Apostles, with their respective symbols. The triptych was intended to be opened only on feast days and holy days, and the side panels were designed to be closed on normal occasions, and had paintings on their reverse side as well.

The triptych has been painted over several times. The first time was during the 1680s, when the fashion for baroque was at its height. The triptych was given a frame of the ubiquitous acanthus leaves [the leaves are now in the Bergen Museum of Cultural History] and surmounted by a Crucifixion group. At the foot of the triptych stands the coat of arms of Inspector-in-Chief of Customs Hans Christopher Hjort and his wife Anna Maria Heidemann, which suggests that they may have paid for the decorations. Today the triptych has been restored to its former condition, with the original magnificent colours.

The pulpit, from 1676, is considered to be the finest piece of baroque furniture in the country. It was greatly admired by contemporaries; when Christian V visited the church in 1685 he did so in order to see for himself "the beauty of the well appointed pulpit". According to the donation tablet it was given to the church by a group of merchants from Bryggen, the Hanseatic wharf. But its artistic provenance is something of a mystery. The use of tortoiseshell and lacquer is different from anything else found in Norway, and indicates a connection with the Far East, perhaps with a country like Holland.

The creator of the 15 life-size figures in the choir, however, is known to have been Søffren Oellsen from Odense, in Denmark. These colourful sculptures represent the Twelve Apostles together with Moses, John the Baptist, and St. Paul.

The church has another unusual feature in the seventeenth- and eighteenth-century portraits that decorate the walls. Most of them are memorial tablets to pastors and prominent citizens of the parish, many of whom are buried under the nave. In addition to German and Dutch painters, the Norwegian painter Elias Fiigenschoug is also represented. Fiigenschoug was responsible for introducing a strong baroque influence into the Bergen school of painting.

BRYGGEN [THE HANSEATIC WHARF]

Bryggen, with its medieval atmosphere and row of pointed gables along the harbour front, has helped to make Bergen known far beyond the frontiers of Norway. For a long time Bryggen was known as the German Wharf, which was something of a misnomer, for it was Norwegian merchants who first established themselves there.

Bergen rose early to prominence as an administrative centre for church and monarchy, and its mild climate and favourable position soon made it a thriving centre for domestic and foreign trade. The first German traders arrived towards the end of the twelfth century; they bought and sold their wares and spent the summer there, returning home at the beginning of the autumn. By about the middle of the thir-

teenth century they had begun to remain in town for the winter, renting accommodation in the houses along the wharf. Soon they began buying up the wharfhouses, and gradually established a branch of the Hanseatic League in Bergen. They gradually gained control over the import of salt and corn, and thus of the whole of the trade with northern Norway including the most important Norwegian export article – dried fish.

As the power and influence of the League began to decline at the end of the fifteenth century, the Hanseatic merchants in Bergen began to be supplanted by Norwegians, who had for several hundred years been living on the other side of the harbour. Gradually the houses on Bryggen changed hands, and were taken over by Norwegian families or Germans who had taken Norwegian nationality. Other immigrants, from England, Scotland, and Holland, were also making their influence felt, and together they ended the German hegemony which had been so strong, and at times so resented.

The red cock has crowed many times in the course of Bergen's history, and although the fire

rooms for eating and drinking and other activities, can be traced back to Norse times. It was adopted and Germanified by the Hanseatic merchants, and in time became associated with them. Each wharfhouse represented a separate small community, consisting of the merchant and his household, clerks and apprentices, servants and so on, and each had its own assembly room. Here, in addition to eating, drinking, and feasting, schooling was given and religious services were held. Since each wharfhouse had its own internal laws and system of government, internal disputes and infringements were tried in the assembly room by an internally appointed tribunal. The most important item of furniture in the assembly room was the long table that ran down the centre. All the activities of the assembly took place around the table, which was also used for corporal punishment, disobedient apprentices being bent over it to be whipped. The beer mugs were hung beneath its rim, and the beer jug, candlesticks, firelighting utensils, and board games had their appointed places on its broad surface.

Next door to the assembly rooms was the bakehouse, or kitchen, where the food was prepared. Each *schøtstue* had its own separate part of the workbench, and to some extent its own cooking utensils. There was a special set of regulations for the kitchen, which had to be posted on the wall and visible at all times, and which contained stringent provisions concerning fire-fighting equipment. Some of these provisions come from the town statutes of 1276, many years before the Hanseatic period.

The most usual route of entry to Bergen for hundreds of years has been the sea, and Bryggen, which was once the largest collection of joined wooden buildings in Europe, must have been an impressive sight to greet the wayfarer sailing into the harbour. It is now on UNESCO's World Heritage List, and forms an attractive part of the city centre, with its small shops, arts and crafts workshops, galleries and restaurants.

regulations were stringent, the houses of Bryggen have suffered a series of damaging fires, the last as late as 1955. Nor did they survive the Middle Ages; the oldest buildings date from after the fire of 1702, when they were rebuilt in the medieval style which had served so well.

In 1872 a merchant called J. W. Olsen was much ridiculed for taking the extraordinary step of leaving the interiors in part of his Bryggen property as they were, and moving his commercial activities into the building next door. The Finne Building, as the property was called, was a so-called "double building", consisting of a double row of rooms behind each other with a narrow passage between. All the wharfhouses were designed in this way, some as double and some as single buildings. The rooms were made of notched logs and built on to each other, with the storerooms on the ground floor and the living and business quarters of the merchants and their households above, with the finest room facing onto the harbour.

Behind the wharfhouses lay the *schøtstuene*, the assembly rooms. This custom, of common

THE FJORDS

Once upon a time, there was a man called Fridtjof. He was braver than other men, and good at all forms of sport, and he was very handsome. He was therefore called Fridtjof the Bold. Fridtjof fell in love with Ingeborg, daughter of King Bele of Balestrand, but Ingeborg's brothers, however, would have none of this; they sent her suitor packing, burned down his farm, and married their sister to the powerful King Ring of Ringerike. Fridtjof then disguised himself and made friends with the king, later becoming his adviser.

When the king died, Fridtjof inherited both Ingeborg and the whole of the kingdom.

This love story, which is probably not true, is told in one of the Icelandic sagas of the fourteenth century. It caught the imagination of Kaiser Wilhelm II. The Kaiser had lost his heart to the fjords of western Norway on his first journey there in 1889, and he returned year after year. No other tourist has left such traces of his visit as Kaiser Wilhelm, and in 1913 he had a 12 metre-high statue of Fridtjof the Bold erected at Vangsnes, on the Sognefjord. And there he stands today, towering on his 14 metre-high pedestal, gazing across the fjord at a statue of King Bele of Balestrand, also put up by the Kaiser.

But the Norwegian fjords had been discovered long before Kaiser Wilhelm's time. Snorre's Saga, written in the thirteenth century, gives detailed descriptions of the sea routes of the time, where the fjords provided many natural harbours and protection from storms. Here, too, a warship could hide and ambush an enemy, or be attacked and ambushed in its turn, as happened to Erling Skjalgsson, a Viking chieftain and supporter of King Canute of England, who followed the king to Norway and met his death in a battle with Olav Haraldsson in the Boknafjord.

Since then the fjords have been regularly visited in peacetime and in war. Travellers who came to the west coast of Norway to trade penetrated further and further up the fjords, and during the nineteenth century the word began to spread that the Norwegian fjords were worth visiting. In spite of harsh and primitive conditions, foreign visitors continued to make admiring journeys, especially the British, who, with their love of nature and of sport, were already familiar with the Norwegian valleys and their wonderful opportunities for salmon-fishing. Around 1850 steamship routes began to be opened up, and these were later supplemented by private steamers carrying wealthy Englishmen, which steamed up the fjords to the great irritation of the salmon-fishers in the inner reaches of the fjords, where the salmon rivers flowed into the sea.

In June 1882 the S/S
Ceylon anchored in Molde
harbour, on her first pleasure cruise up the west
coast to the North Cape.
She was the first of many,
and it was no coincidence
that many of these ships bo-
re the names of kings.
Among the crowned heads
that made this marvellous
scenic voyage up the coast
were King Oscar II of Sweden and Norway, King Leo-
pold of the Belgians, the
King of Siam, and of course
Kaiser Wilhelm.

The British and the Ger-
mans between them also
made the name of the Jøs-
sing fjord known during the
Second World War through
the Altmark incident. In February 1940, before the
Norwegians had entered the
war, the German auxiliary
cruiser *Altmark*, carrying
the captured Allied crews of several merchant
vessels, sought refuge in the Jøssing fjord, where
it was cornered by the English destroyer
Cossack. The *Altmark* ran aground and the *Cossack* was able to rescue the 299 British sailors on
board. The term "jøssing" came to be used by
the Nazis as an insult and by the Norwegians as
a compliment.

"When one hears the word Hardanger, one
immediately thinks of something delightful,"
wrote the nineteenth-century painter Hans Gude. The Hardanger fjord branches out into innumerable inlets and arms, each with its own
beauty. Not even the pictures in the tourist brochures of jagged, snow-capped mountains, of
foaming waterfalls crashing hundreds of feet into
the blue depths of the fjord below, and of
glimpses of the white lace and pale pink tracery
of the fruit blossom, can convey the full impact

of the scenery of Hardanger, or of the beauty of
a place like Ullensvang, with its medieval church
and the glittering glacier of Folgefonni in the
background. At the peak of the romantic movement in the last century artists flocked to the
shores of Hardanger to immortalize it, and in
their wake came the tourists. Norway's longest
fjord is the Sognefjord, which stretches 205 kilometres inland, passing many of the main tourist
attractions of western Norway along its length.
The Geiranger fjord is also well known and is
considered by many to be the most beautiful of
the fjords, with its Alpine landscape. But Norwegian fjords are not only found along the west
coast; the whole seaboard, from Sweden in the
east to the Russian border in the north, is cleft
and intersected by innumerable tongues of water
and rocky outcrops, each with its own un-
deniable character and atmosphere.

ORGUND STAVE CHURCH

With a "flaming torch" in one hand and some dried juniper twigs in the other, Gjertrud Johannesdotter Tråe walked, with a firm, determined step, towards the church. One of the other women of the village, Sissel Kallevang, saw her and was frightened. Surely mad Gjertrud couldn't be going to set fire to the church? She had always been dangerous, but it was true that she seemed to have become worse since her husband's death, eight years before. Sissel shouted out, and Gjertrud began to run. Once inside the church she pushed her twigs under the confessional and lit them, and soon wisps of smoke were curling up under the roof. But Sissel's cries brought the other villagers out in force, and the church was saved.

Gjertrud, despite her madness, was tried and convicted. She was furious: was she not to be able to cook herself a little soup, she, a poor woman who was not allowed even to receive the sacrament at mass? This incident took place at midsummer in 1782. Once again St. Andrew, to whom the church was dedicated, had averted

the hand of fate, just as he had done ever since the church was first built, at the end of the twelfth century.

Of the 32 preserved stave churches, Heddal in Telemark is the largest, Urnes, on the edge of the Lusterfjord, is the oldest, and Borgund, in Lærdal, is the best preserved. Apart from a few small changes, its appearance is still the same as when it was first built. The church has a nave, aisles, a choir and an apse. The many roofs are covered with shingles, and the outside is impregnated with tar. The whole building

is surrounded by a romanesque gallery, with carved portals on the west and south sides. The decoration of the west portal is particularly characteristic of the period: dragon-like beasts engaged in battle, entwined with tendrils in fluid rhythmic undulations.

The architectonic complexity of the exterior of the church, with roof rising above roof to the gables surmounted with snarling dragon's heads, and the slim, delicate spire crowning all, is in strong contrast to the simplicity of the interior. This is dominated by the staves, or pillars, that support the main arch of the roof and divide the space into a high rectangular central section and narrow, lower aisles along the outer walls. These staves are the main structural element, which give the church its name. Another interesting detail is that not a bolt or a nail in the entire building, either outside or inside, is made of metal – they are all of pinewood.

The interior decorations are also simple, which is understandable considering the darkness of the church. In the "Visitors' guide" published by the Society for the Preservation of Norwegian Ancient Monuments in 1898, there is the following description:

"When the doors are closed, we find ourselves suddenly plunged into almost complete darkness, which is made even greater by contrast with the occasional ray of light from the original window in the west gable or from the small openings high up on the side walls. If must be remembered, however, that in those days the service consisted only of a short mass in front of the altar in artificial light, and that there was no real need to light up the body of the church where the congregation stood, since there were no hymn books."

The altar, where the holy vessels of silver gilt or copper shone brilliantly in the light of candles and tapers, must have stood out as a focus in the dark interior, and the congregation's concentration on the word of God and the actions of the priest must have been intense. The congregation always stood during the service, and the bench along the wall was only intended for the sick

and elderly.

Today there is nothing left of the original furnishings – the altarpiece is from the beginning of the seventeenth century, the pulpit from the second half of the sixteenth. However, there are runes carved on the outer and inner walls, which have been dated to the twelfth century, when the church was built. One of these, which runs "God help everyone who helps me to make a journey", may reflect a desire to make a pilgrimage, perhaps northwards to see the coffin of St. Olav in Nidaros Cathedral.

wonderful view of the splendour of Trollveggen. The Kaiser would sit here for hours, examining the towers and spires of Trolltindene through his field glasses. The Norwegian writer and nature-lover Theodor Caspari, who encountered the Kaiser there in 1904, described him as being "spellbound by this most dramatic point in the Norwegian landscape".

The Norwegian landscape *is* dramatic, changeable, and full of mystery. Its extraordinary mountainous rock formations, especially, have given rise to many myths and legends. Trolls were frequently turned to stone on these mountain slopes when they encountered stronger opponents, which sometimes took the form of St. Olav and sometimes of the sun's rays, which it is well known no troll can tolerate. The pointed peaks of Trolltindene are thus the remains of all the trolls who were turned to stone by King Olav the Holy when they tried to prevent him from bringing the glad news of the White Christ over the mountains to Romsdalen in 1028.

In 1936 another king went the same way, although on a somewhat different errand. King Haakon VII was to officiate at the ceremonial opening of the new Trollstigveien between Sylte in Valldalen valley and Åndalsnes. That this fantastic piece of road was ever finished was a feat of magic in itself. It took 100 men 20 years to build the road, struggling all the way against the waterfalls that cascaded down the mountainside. Starting from Sylte, we can follow the path of Olav the Holy for some way, passing Olavshelleren, or Olav's Rock, where he camped with his men the night before his famous action in clearing the way so that men could pass Skjærsura. This was a pile of rocky debris that had always proved impassible, and the king had been warned by the farmers of Sylte that it was no use trying to pass that way. Refusing to give up, Olav put his 400 men to work on clearing the rubble and mobilized another hundred farmers and their horses to help. Even so, they were forced to give up. Then, says Snorre in his saga, "the king took off his cloak and said that they should all come and try once more, and this was done. And now

*T*ROLLSTIGEN [THE PATH OF THE TROLLS]

Many a visitor has fallen under the spell of Trolltindene, the mighty and inaccessible mountain range between the valleys of Romsdalen and Isterdalen. It was one of the favourite views of Kaiser Wilhelm II, who on his annual trip along the west coast of Norway would anchor the royal yacht *Hohenzollern* at Veblungsnes, whence the royal party would proceed by landauer to the posting station Horgheim. Horgheim lies at the foot of the Romsdalshorn, and provides a twenty men moved stones as far as was necessary that one hundred men had not even managed to lift before, and the path was cleared before the evening meal, so that there was a passage for both men and packhorses, as good as if the ground had been flat." And the stream by Olav's Rock, where they had paused for refreshment, became a source of healing for both men and animals after the king had washed himself in it.

The 56 kilometre-long Trollstigen reaches its highest point 850 metres above sea level. There is a viewing platform at Stigrøra, which can be reached by a path, which provides a magnificent view of the peaks of Karitind, Dronningen [the Queen], Kongen [the King], and Bispen [the Bishop] to the west, and of the 11 hairpin bends of the road that winds down to Stigfoss bridge and the valley of Isterdalen. The old pack road can also be seen, marked by white stones. The Stigfossen waterfall, which has a total fall of 320 metres and an almost completely perpendicular fall of 40 metres, sends a refreshing spray of water drops over the travellers passing by. Tverrdalsfossen is another of the Trollstigen waterfalls, with an even longer fall.

The jagged peaks of Trolltindene on the eastern side of Isterdalen are probably the most impressive rock formations in the whole of Norway. They form a more or less unbroken range of pinnacles and crags interspersed with dizzying abysses. One of the many legends tells that the trolls had been holding a wedding feast, and that they celebrated not wisely but too well. Before they realized what was happening, the sun had risen, and the whole wedding party was turned to stone. And there they still are: Trollgubben [the Troll], Trollkjerringa [the Troll Woman], the Bride, the Bridegroom, and the Best Man.

ÆLESUND

"No other town in this country sticks out into the sea like Ålesund does. It lies here beneath our feet like a fish hook in the North Sea, a long thin stretch of stoney pebbles, of heavy, cement-grey houses around harbours and sounds, clinging to every rock on the shore and rising and falling with every bump in the ground." The writer Arthur Klæbo's description of his home town Ålesund was made as he looked down on it from the heights of Aksla – like so many Norwegian towns, Ålesund can be viewed from a nearby rise. He also speculated on the origin of the town: "... the town rose straight out of the ocean one stormy day out of sheer contrariness."

There is no doubt that the best possible place to catch one's first sight of Ålesund is from the viewpoint Kniven, or the Knife, on the hill of Aksla, which rises from the middle of the town. Here one can see how the town jumps from island to island until it ends far out among the Atlantic breakers, against a backdrop formed by the jagged mountain peaks of Sunnmøre.

Snorre's saga tells how Olav the Holy anchored at Steinvåg, as Ålesund was called in those days. At that time, between Spjelkavik and what is today the centre of Ålesund, lay the town of Borgundkaupang, the most important ecclesiastical and commercial centre in the district of Sunnmøre. However, during the fourteenth and fifteenth centuries the fortunes of Borgundkaupang declined with the drop in Hanseatic trade, and

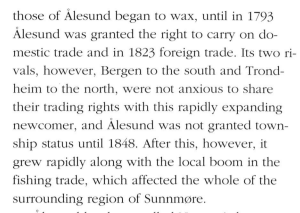

those of Ålesund began to wax, until in 1793 Ålesund was granted the right to carry on domestic trade and in 1823 foreign trade. Its two rivals, however, Bergen to the south and Trondheim to the north, were not anxious to share their trading rights with this rapidly expanding newcomer, and Ålesund was not granted township status until 1848. After this, however, it grew rapidly along with the local boom in the fishing trade, which affected the whole of the surrounding region of Sunnmøre.

Ålesund has been called Norway's largest fishing village, and there is some truth in the name. Fish were the foundation for the wealth of the town, as its coat of arms indicates: a combined fishing and cargo boat in full sail with three fish. As late as the 1950s the town was said to be "so teeming with fish, fishermen, and boats that it resembled a modern Klondyke". And fish is still very much a part of Ålesund today. It is bisected by the Brosundet canal with its picturesque fishing harbour, which is always full of fishing smacks selling newly caught fish and shellfish to those who do not prefer to fish their own straight from the edge of the wharf. The town also has an aquarium, where the fish and other marine life are shown as far as possible in their natural environment. Ålesund exports dried cod in enormous quantities all over the world, and the favourite dish of the people of Ålesund is none other than the Portuguese national dish bacalhao.

At the beginning of the present century Ålesund, like so many Norwegian towns, consisted almost entirely of wooden houses clustered together along narrow streets; there were no more than four or five buildings made of masonry in the whole town. But on the night of 22 January 1904, in the teeth of a hurricane, the premises of Ålesund Preserving Company caught fire. The flames spread mercilessly, and given the force of the wind there was little the fire brigade could do. Out of a total of 1050 houses, only about 250 were left standing. Ten thousand people were made homeless, although extraordinarily enough only one life was lost. Help came pouring into

the town after the disaster, and not only from the state and municipality, but from all over the country and even from abroad. The very next day the writer Alexander Kielland, governor of Molde, arrived in Ålesund on board the *Rauma*, laden with food and clothes for the survivors, and Kaiser Wilhelm himself sent the *Prinz Heinrich* with a cargo of supplies and building materials.

Within three years the centre of the town had been rebuilt, in the contemporary style known as "Jugendstil" or art nouveau. The style took different forms in different countries, and in Ålesund it was influenced by the Norwegian dragon style. The result was highly decorative, with imaginative scrolls and curves, full of architectonic details like spires and towers. Thanks to the fire, Ålesund is today one of the few preserved towns in Jugenstil, and in 1988 it received a national prize, the Houens Memorial Prize, for the conservation of its unique urban centre.

THE BIRD SANCTUARY AT RUNDE

Precipices interspersed with clefts and crannies, crags and cliffs, grottoes and needle-sharp points of rock, carved out by the action of the waves – this is Runde, the outermost inhabited island of the Herøy group, west of Ålesund. One hundred and fifty people live on Runde, making their living by fishing, as pilots, and by manning the lighthouse. The island also has a good harbour. Runde's fame, however, is due to Rundebranden, on the north-west side of the island, which is the most easily accessible and one of the largest of the nesting cliffs for vast colonies of seabirds that are found up and down the Norwegian coast, from Stavanger to Finnmark. The cliff rises a perpendicular 300 metres straight up from the sea, an avian Tower of Babel where hundreds of thousands of seabirds, each with its own special cry, are staking claims and defending territory. Here we find kittiwake, guillemot, razorbill, cormorant, and puffin, to name some of the most common.

The kittiwake, a gull about the size of the common seagull, is the most numerous of the species nesting on Rundebranden, which has one of the largest colonies in the country. The puffin, or sea parrot, as it is also known, comes a good second, followed by the shag. A welcome latecomer to the cliff is the petrel, which first established nesting colonies on Runde during the 1920–30s, the first place in Norway where the bird began nesting. It obviously thrived here, since the nesting colony now numbers over a thousand birds, and petrels have also begun to nest on other islands on this part of the coast. Another less common species is the gannet, which was first observed nesting in Norway in 1946, here on Rundebranden, and has established a relatively large colony since then. The rare skua is also increasing in numbers. There are altogether 32 species that are definitely known to nest on the cliff, and a further 11 that are thought to nest here.

The various species utilize all parts of the cliff, which resembles nothing so much as a block of flats, with different species occupying various floors and having different requirements as regards comfort and convenience. Puffins prefer the ground floor; they like to nest in a scree or to lay their eggs in turf or earth, where they can dig deep holes. The razor-bill and guillemot, on the other hand, make few demands as regards a home, depositing their eggs under a convenient stone or in a crack in the sheer cliffside. The kittiwake also likes steep cliffs, but permits itself the luxury of proper nests built of straw and seaweed. The visitor can follow a path up to the top of the island, where there are notices directing visitors to observation posts where they can get a good view of the sites of the various colonies. Be-

tween 15 March and 31 August it is prohibited to climb the nesting cliff itself or to land there from a boat, so as not to disturb the birds.

Not only is Rundebranden a bird sanctuary, but the whole island has been made into a nature reserve. The beaches along the south and western sides of the island swarm with different varieties of birds, including oyster catchers, eider duck, shelduck, lapwing and many other waders, besides colonies of small birds. Over 200 species have been observed on the island. Besides the bird life, all flora is protected, and the island has several rare species of plants, some of which are threatened. The pebbled beaches along the eastern side are especially rich in rare plants such as the poisonous crowfoot.

In addition to its natural treasures, Runde has been known for several hundred years as a more conventional treasure island. On the night of 2 March 1725, the Dutch East Indiaman *Akerendam* sank off the coast, with a cargo of, among other things, 230,000 florins on board. Only five of the 19 money chests were recovered, but in 1972–73 many of the coins were retrieved and can be seen in the Collection of Coins and Medals at the Historical Museum in Oslo.

THE COASTAL STEAMER

One of the most spectacular sea voyages in the world is undoubtedly the 12,500 kilometres from Bergen to Kirkenes. Every day of the year the 11 coastal steamers are to be found somewhere along this coast, steaming past some of the most beautiful scenes in the whole of Norway, a country with more than its fair share of beautiful

scenery – rows of snow-clad peaks, fjords and glaciers, nesting cliffs aswarm with birds, reindeer herds and fisheries, the midnight sun and the northern lights. Although the ships are admirably equipped to carry tourists on pleasure cruises up and down the coast, their primary purpose is to fulfil the demands of ordinary coastal traffic, carrying passengers, cargo, and mail from place to place between 35 large and small ports of call. The further north one goes, the more important the role played by the coastal steamer in people's daily lives. Whatever the time of day, when the coastal steamer calls in port there is usually a crowd waiting, to welcome new arrivals, to see people off, or simply to keep an eye on what is happening.

There has always been a constant and regular traffic between Bergen and the north of Norway. The sea route was one of the easiest and most practical in a country seamed and cleft by deep fjords and impassible mountains. Ships would sail south heavily laden with dried cod, and returned northwards with cargoes of such necessities as salt, sugar, flour and household articles. During the 1830s the first steamship, the *Prinds Gustav*, began to sail up and down the coast, to the dismay of traditionalists and the

great satisfaction of those who believed in progress. Gradually a regular traffic grew up along the northern part of the coast, with scheduled arrivals and departures, but since the steamers put into port at night, the journey took a very long time, and even in the summer the boats only called once a week.

This situation continued until the captain of the *Vesteraalen*, Richard With, decided that it must be possible to sail during the night. He allied himself with the legendary pilot Anders Holte, and together they made plans for sailing in the dark using compasses, maps, lighthouses, and carefully noted observations. The authorities considered the plans to be pure madness, and no insurance company could be found to insure the ship. In spite of these difficulties, on 2 July 1893 a flag-bedecked *Vesteraalen* sailed out of Trondheim harbour with Captain With at the helm on course for Hammerfest. The journey took three days, and was a regular triumphal progress northwards; at every port of call, whatever the time of day, people flocked to the quay and celebrated the ship's arrival. For the people of northern Norway this marked an end to their comparative isolation and a significant improvement in communications.

Now the coastal steamer runs on a daily schedule all the year round, on both the northbound and the south-bound routes, and has done so since 1936. It was not long before the route became a tourist attraction, and it is the large numbers of tourists that keep it going today from Bergen to Kirkenes. During the

summer the ships are crowded with travellers from all corners of the world, who, in addition to the magnificent scenery, are able to experience for themselves how postal services and transport of goods are carried on in a country with a scattered population spread over very large distances. Even in the winter there are tourists, who are coming in increasing numbers to sample the attractions of winter in Norway – the mysterious glow and flimmer of the northern lights, a forest of masts belonging to the fishing fleet around the Lofoten islands, sparkling white peaks against an icy blue midwinter sky. Many travellers swear by their own ship, and always take care to make the journey on that particular steamer.

The entire journey from Bergen to Kirkenes and back takes 12 days. For many people the North Cape is the high point of the voyage, for others the western fjords. But each part of the coastline has its own special charm, and each port of call its individual attraction. Many would agree, however, that few experiences can match passing through the narrow sound of Rørvik and into the channel of Nordlandsleia, where one enters a world of fairy-tales and trolls. The fantastic nature of the scenery here has inspired many tales of mystery and imagination, of giants and giantesses and trolls. One of the best known has given the names to the mountains round about.

After passing the mountain of Hestmannen, the steamer crosses the Arctic Circle and enters the land of the midnight sun.

NIDAROS CATHEDRAL

"Even before nones people were already streaming towards Christchurch, carrying and supporting their sick and crippled so as to find a place for them in the nave, whence they could be near the coffin as it was borne out in the procession on the next day after mass." "The next day" was the vigil of St. Olav, and it was thus that the writer and Nobel Prize winner Sigrid Undset describes her heroine, Kristin Lavransdatter's, first meeting with Christchurch or Nidaros Cathedral, for the town of Trondheim was called Nidaros during the Middle Ages.

For all over Norway, and from all over Europe, pilgrims flocked to Christchurch, where St. Olav, *rex perpetuus norvegiae*, or Norway's eternal king, lay buried in his silver coffin up by the high altar. This church, with the coffin of St. Olav and the legendary spring of St. Olav with its healing water, was one of the most famous places of pilgrimage during the Middle Ages; only Jerusalem, Rome, and Santiago de Compostella attracted greater numbers of pilgrims.

In his struggle to convert Norway to Christianity, King Olav Haraldsson was killed by an enemy at the Battle of Stiklestad on 29 July 1030. A farmer called Torgils Holmesån and his son Grim buried the king's body in secret in a sandy bank beside a river some way south of Stiklestad. After a short time miracles and other mysterious happenings began to take place near the grave, and when the king's body was dug up, a year later, it was quite free from any sign of decay, and the hair and nails were seen to have grown. Snorre's saga also says that "On the sandbank, where King Olav had lain in the earth, a clear spring welled up, and people were healed from their sickness by this water". Olav's Well, or Olav's Spring, is now in the cathedral, and the high altar now stands above what is thought to be the site of the king's first grave.

No one knows where King Olav lies buried now. During the centuries after his death, the king's body was moved continuously from one hiding place to another. When, however, on the initiation of Bishop Grimkjell, the king was sanctified, his body was placed in a costly coffin and remained peacefully in the cathedral throughout the rest of the Middle Ages. With the Reformation the veneration of saints was abolished, and Archbishop Olav Engelbrektsson fled, taking the coffin and its contents with him, to his castle at Steinviksholm. Here he was pursued by the Danish king's men, who smashed open the coffin and sent the silver and precious stones south to Copenhagen. The king was provisionally buried in the graveyard of a small church in North Trøndelag county, before again being transported to Nidaros Cathedral for burial. But it is not known whereabouts in the cathedral his grave lies: the whole choir and the octagon are full of graves. It is now thought that the most likely site of Olav's grave is a corner of the crypt below the pulpit.

Nidaros Cathedral is the largest medieval building in the Nordic countries. It has a total length of 100 metres, a transept measuring 50

metres, and a height at the highest point of 21 metres. The building was probably begun by St. Olav's nephew, Olav Kyrre, the same king who founded Bergen. The oldest part of the church, the transept, is one of the finest examples of romanesque architecture in the country. It was begun during the first half of the twelfth century and completed in a transitional style between romanesque and gothic by Archbishop Eystein in about 1161. When the archbishop returned home in 1183 after three years in exile, he had become familiar with the great gothic cathedrals of Continental Europe. New building work was started, this time in the continental gothic style. The ribbed vaulting in the small Chapter House on the north side of the church is probably the first of its kind in Norway. The choir and the remarkable and unique octagon were also built in the new style.

The cathedral not only pioneered a new style of architecture, it was also a contemporary centre of plastic art; the statue of St. John, dated about 1270, which stands in the west front, is considered the most remarkable, and most European, work of Norwegian high gothic.

Fire has ravaged the cathedral five times, that of 1531 acting as a kind of overture to the depredations of the Reformation in 1536, when the Danish king allowed the church to be plundered of its treasures. A comprehensive work of restoration and rebuilding began in 1869, and has been going on to a varying extent ever since.

The cathedral has been decorated by a number of well-known Norwegian artists of the present century. When the sun shines through the great rose window by Gabriel Kielland, it is difficult not to think of a description from the sixteenth century. Then, too, there was "a great rose made of stone, which was completely gilded and in it was set a great carbuncle, so that when the sun shone, no one could gaze on it with their eyes, so brightly did it shine".

Nidaros Cathedral has been the seat of many ceremonial occasions. On 22 June 1907 Haakon VII was crowned king of a free and independent Norway. Here, too, 52 years later to the day, his son Olav was consecrated, and on 23 June 1991 King Olav's son, Harald, and his wife Sonja were also consecrated as King and Queen of Norway.

AUSTRÅT

In Ørlandet, not far from Trondheim, with a broad view over the fjord, towers an ancient castle in "a bare and dreadful landscape". This is Austråt, the farm that faces east, the seventeenth-century home of Ove Bjelke, chancellor of the realm. Over the entrance to the tower is a Latin inscription: "This building has, with God's help, been left by Ove Bjelke to his descendants to take care of."

In a country of farmhouses and log cabins, but very few large stone buildings or castles, Ove Bjelke must have been proud of his castle-like edifice. But if it had not been for his second wife, Regitze Gedde, he would probably have been satisfied with the more modest wooden farmhouse that had been in the family for years. Regitze, however, was the daughter of Admiral Ove Gedde, and made unfavourable comparisons between Austråt and her father's house in

southern Norway near Tønsberg, which was called Sem. The stable at Sem, said Regitze, was a much finer building than the main house at Austråt.

Understandably, the governor was highly incensed by these insinuations, and pulled down the old wooden fort which had been the seat of his great great grandmother, the stalwart Fru Inger, and her family since the fifteenth century. In its place he built a mansion in a mixture of renaissance and baroque, which

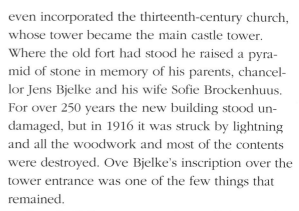

even incorporated the thirteenth-century church, whose tower became the main castle tower. Where the old fort had stood he raised a pyramid of stone in memory of his parents, chancellor Jens Bjelke and his wife Sofie Brockenhuus. For over 250 years the new building stood undamaged, but in 1916 it was struck by lightning and all the woodwork and most of the contents were destroyed. Ove Bjelke's inscription over the tower entrance was one of the few things that remained.

It took Bjelke two years, from 1654 to 1656, to build Austråt. After the fire his descendants did their best, but it took 40 years, from 1920 to 1961, for them to restore it to its present condition. Bjelke would probably have enjoyed seeing how much of the taxpayer's money went into restoring his castle; at any rate, he must feel a debt of gratitude to Ibsen for reviving the name of his great great grandmother Fru Inger in his play *Fru Inger til Østråt* [Mistress Inger of Østråt, or Austråt] of 1857. Since then the personalities of its owners and its grand and romantic setting have fascinated many Norwegian writers.

From the early Middle Ages Austråt has been the seat of powerful chieftans. The farm is mentioned in Olav Tryggvason's saga, which tells how one Skjegge Asbjørnson, known as Iron-Beard, fell in 999 in battle against Olav Tryggvason and was buried in a burial mound at Austråt. But the name most closely associated with Austråt is that of Inger Ottersdatter Rømer, who lived in about 1475–1555. Fru Inger married Nils Henrikssøn Gyldenløve, member of the Rigsråd, or Council, was widowed at an early age and governed Austråt with an iron hand. It was not a small property she had to administer; she was the largest landowner in the country, possessing no less than one-seventh of the territory of Norway. It was said of her that her desire for possessions was limitless, that she made claims on property she had little right to, and that she sacrificed her own daughters on the altar of wealth. She was a ceaseless intriguer, in politics as well as otherwise, but she did much to foster Norwegian independence under the Danish-Norwegian

union. In the game of power politics alliances were formed and re-formed constantly, and one of Fru Inger's closest allies, Archbishop Olaf Engelbrektsson, of Nidaros [the old name for Trondheim] became a sworn enemy. He helped to murder two of her sons-in-law, Nils Lykke and Vincents Lunge, and even managed to have her expelled for a while from Austråt. Fru Inger, who had a weakness for the new Lutheran faith, must have enjoyed the archbishop's discomfiture when the Reformation drove him into exile. But the archbishop had the last word: as he left he had Austråt looted.

Although Fru Inger made her estate over to her son-in-law Jens Bjelke in her old age, defending her property continued to preoccupy her, and ironically enough was the cause of her death. In 1555 she set out for Bergen together with her daughter Lucie and her granddaughter Gundel to "defend her property at the Thing".

On the way the ship was caught in a storm and sank, and everyone on board was drowned. The bodies were buried locally, and Ove Bjelke had the sarcophagi placed in a chapel he built in memory of the family.

This brings us back to Ove Bjelke's Austråt. Bjelke was a much-travelled man, who had studied law at Padua and had visited Vienna and Madrid. Thus it was not without reason that Austråt has been called "a strange southern flower in the windblown desert of Ørlandet". The square complex of buildings around an upper and a lower courtyard was inspired by southern Europe, and has no parallel in Norwegian architecture or building styles. Completely un-Norwegian, too, is the main entrance to the castle, the Sea Gate, which is surmounted by the family coats of arms.

THE GROTTOES OF RANA

Limestone grottoes, with their stalactites and stalagmites, subterranean lakes and frozen waterfalls, are not common in Scandinavia, but the mountain of Tosenfjellet in Rana district contains many hundreds. In fact 75 per cent of all the grottoes in this part of Europe are found in Nordland county.

In many parts of the world grottoes and caves are fairly common, and most of them are to be found in areas with a good deal of limestone. Limestone consists mainly of calcite, or calcium carbonate, which dissolves relatively easily in water, especially if the water is carbonated. Thus caves and grottoes are often found in the neighbourhood of rivers or dried-up river beds, or along the coast where the sea has dissolved the limestone in chalk cliffs.

Norway has few areas where limestone is a dominating rock stratum, but one of the largest is Nordland county. The limestone here was formed between the Cambrian and Silurian periods, 400 to 500 million years ago, perhaps as coral reefs or banked-up shell deposits in a tropical sea. During the Silurian–Devonian transi-

tion period, about 400 million years ago, these rock formations were folded and crushed by the movement of the earth's crust to form the types of rock we find today, the metamorphosed limestone in the form of marble and mica slate.

During the deformation of the earth's crust to form mountains, the rocks were fractured and became seamed with cracks, through which ground water could run. When the water ran over rocks that could be dissolved chemically, like marble and limestone, this started a long process of hollowing out and carving up. Running through the cracks in the rock, the water enlarges them and makes room for more water, and so on. If the water is carbonated, the

process goes faster. The cracks gradually become clefts, and through these streams, swelling into rivers, find their way underground, until they form a whole system of underground rivers. The rivers carry with them stones and gravel from above ground, and pebbles transported for long distances have often been found in potholes.

There are about 800 grottoes and caves of all sizes and shapes in Nordland county, and new ones are continually being discovered. Most of them are not accessible and should not be attempted by amateurs, but two grottoes are open to the public. The best known of these is Grønli grotto, which has about 10,000 visitors a year. The grotto stretches about 250 metres into the mountain, and has a river running through it, creating an eery magical atmo-

sphere with its runs and waterfalls. The strange rock formations can be seen by artificial light and in the part known as the Chapel lies a huge block of granite. It is a mystery how this rock came to be in the cave, because the nearest seam of granite is many kilometres away. It may be that the block was borne along by a glacier, which pressed it into the grotto on its way down the valley, or it may have been washed in by the ice during its retreat about 10,000 years ago. A guided tour around Grønli grotto only lasts 20 minutes and is an interesting experience for the whole family.

Seter grotto, on the other hand, is far more demanding, comprising a two-hour tour of endless underground passages and caves, potholes, vast halls and narrow passages. Here the strange limestone shapes are illuminated by patches of chalk-white marble, making the tour an unforgettable experience.

All the grottoes in the Rana area are listed for protection.

THE ARCTIC CIRCLE CENTRE – 66°33' NORTH

The Arctic Circle is only a line drawn on a map, and yet it marks an important boundary. Frontiers between countries are also lines on maps, but who has not felt some excitement when crossing from a familiar to an unknown country? Crossing the Arctic Circle has a sort of mystic significance, like crossing the equator.

During the summer solstice the sun remains above the horizon all day and all night. There are of course two lands of the midnight sun, one north of the Arctic, and one south of the Antarctic Circle. But the climate in the latter cannot support human life for any length of time, and if it were not for the Gulf Stream no one could live above the Arctic Circle either. Thanks to the Norwegian Atlantic current, which branches off from the current passing the British Isles on its way to the Barents Sea and Spitzbergen, the north of Norway has a habitable climate and has been inhabited for thousands of years. It also has a rich indigenous flora and fauna, specially adapted to the long light summer nights.

Until a few years ago the only object to be seen through a car or train window as one cros-

sed the Arctic Circle on the bare and windy upland of Salt-fjellet mountain, was a metal sphere mounted on a small stone plinth. Since 1990 this has been replaced by the impressive and unusual Arctic Circle Centre, a suitable landmark for the transition to a region full of contrasts and new experiences. The building, which has the Arctic Circle run-

ning through it, presents a selection of north Norwegian art, culture, and economic life, and tourist information. There is also an exhibition of stuffed indigenous animals, where a massive polar bear forms the natural high point. A street paved in white marble runs through it, containing shops and a post office with its own postal code: "8242 Polar-sirkelen", which has proved a great attraction for visitors. The number of visitors stopping at the Circle has increased enormously since the Centre opened, and the figure will soon approach that for the North Cape.

The Centre is in the middle of a region inhabited by Sami, and there are traces of habitation in this area as far back as the Bronze Age. The Sami used to be regarded as a mysterious people, and there used to be many myths about their beliefs and customs, about the strange powers of the magic drums of the shamans and about their sacrificial customs. Reindeer were sacrificed, usually bulls, with prayers for good grazing conditions for the herds, protection from wild animals, and high fertility. Sometimes alcoholic liquor was offered up, and in such cases the shaman, or *nåjonen*, as he was called, was occasionally tempted to cheat, by having a small container hidden beneath the sacrificial altar, where the liquid could be collected for his own personal use. Near the Centre is just such an ancient sacrificial altar consisting of three stones, which is now listed as a cultural monument. The Sami still herd reindeer over Saltfjellet, and information can be obtained at the Centre about their culture.

On the Swedish side of the border are the Nasa silver mines; the border was actually moved at one point to make sure that the mines

lay on the Swedish side. At one time the Sami living in the area were grossly exploited and used as slave labour in the mines.

The first landmark showing the location of the Arctic Circle on Saltfjellet was set up here when the road was built in 1937, in the form of a pillar. When the Germans arrived at this point during the invasion of Norway they carved a swastika and the date, 1940, into the pillar. The swastika has since been removed.

The Germans did, however, improve communications; and the railway line to north Norway, which had only reached Mosjøen when the war broke out, was rapidly extended. A large labour force was needed and thousands of Rus-

sian prisoners-of-war were sent to northern Norway for this purpose. They lived under appalling conditions and the local population took many dangerous risks to supply them with food and clothing. In spite of this, 7000 of them died, and are buried in the churchyard at Tjøtta. The memorial raised to these men by their surviving comrades in 1945, was incorporated into the new Centre when it was opened in 1990.

Saltfjellet has many unhappy memories. A further 7000 Jugoslav partisans and political prisoners were sent to Norway to work camps, most of them being collected together on Saltfjellet in "Lager Polarkreis". They, too, have a memorial, which was moved to the Centre when it opened.

THE LOFOTEN ISLANDS

"Dreadful, wild, and totally uninhabitable." This was the description of the landscape of Lofoten given by a traveller's guide published in 1830, and the statement continued to express the general opinion of Lofoten for the next 40 years. Until Norway's national poet, Bjørnstjerne Bjørnson, journeyed up the coast and was lost in enthusiasm at the sight – nothing he had ever seen previously could compare with Lofoten's "wonderful mountains".

But Bjørnson was not the first to be impressed by the scenery of Lofoten. In 1432 The Italian Pietro Quirinius and his crew, sailing from Italy to Flanders, were shipwrecked off the island of Røst, and wrote several descriptions of their stay on the outermost of the Lofoten islands. In 1667 another Italian, Francesco Negri, also visited the islands, and described among other things the amazing method used by the inhabitants of Værøy for catching eagles with their bare hands. This unusual industry was continued right up to the present day, and was only stopped in 1970.

Bjørnson's enthusiastic descriptions attracted the interest of many contemporary artists, who journeyed north to try and capture the landscape and the extraordinary light conditions. Writers, too, have been inspired by the dramatic surroundings and the myths and mystery of these windswept islands.

The range of peaks known as Lofotveggen, the Lofoten Wall, does indeed resemble a wall stretching south-west and out to sea. However, the mountains are not linked, and the archipelago consists of thousands of large and small islands. And in the lee of the mountains are picturesque fishing villages, sheltered harbours, and wonderful sandy beaches.

Lofoten has always lived by and for fishing, and even has separate legislation governing the Lofoten fisheries, and a special judicial system for enforcing it. The season lasts from January to April, and in 1947, the year of the great catch, there were 20,000 fishermen taking part. This is due to the fact that the Arctic cod comes to the banks off Lofoten to spawn in the perfect conditions provided by the Gulf Stream.

Nestling below the harsh mountain peaks are narrow strips of land where agriculture is possible. In spite of the northerly latitude the climate is mild, and grain has been grown here since about the year 2000 BC. At Borg, on the island of Vestvågøy, the site has been found of a chieftain's seat which may have been one of the largest and most important in Scandinavia. It is thought that it may have belonged to Tore Hjort, a Lofoten chieftain who was killed by Olav Tryggvason in the year 998.

Ever since the fifteenth century, however, the export of dried cod has been the most important source of revenue for Lofoten, and most of the population live in fishing villages. Nusfjord, where most of the houses date from the nineteenth century, has been placed on UNESCO's World Heritage List. At the beginning of this century about 350 boats would often row out from Nusfjord, which at this time boasted 60 *rorbuer*, of which 20 have been preserved. The *rorbu* was a wooden shanty where the fishermen slept and lived during the fishing season. In addition to the *rorbuer*, there were facilities for treating the fish and making cod liver oil, a very valuable article of trade, boathouses, and shops. Not far away lies Sund, with its Fisheries Museum and its local artist, Hans Gjertsen, "the blacksmith of Sund", who is famous for his elegant cormorants wrought in steel.

The most characteristic of the fishing villages, however, is Henningsvær, which lies on a tiny island off the coast of the island of Austvågøy. As late as the 1950s there were seldom fewer than 5000 fishermen here during the fishing season, and there was a saying that one could walk dry shod from boat to boat during the fishing. The church, which has stained glass by Victor Sparre, was built in the form of a fish-drying rack in order to fit in with the surroundings. The island had no wheeled traffic until 1983, when a bridge was built connecting it with the mainland.

But the largest and probably the most influential of the fishing villages was Kabelvåg. King Eystein built churches and *rorbuer* here, and Snorre's saga describes the Vågastevnet, as the annual meeting between buyers and sellers of fish became known. By the thirteenth century a small town had grown up. North of Kabelvåg is the Lofoten Cathedral, built in 1898, which with its seating capacity of 1200 people is the largest log-built church north of Trondheim. The Lofoten Museum and the Lofoten Aquarium, with its original design, are also situated in Kabelvåg.

Svolvær is the capital of Lofoten. Ever since Bjørnson's enthusiastic exclamations, this town has possessed a special attraction for artists. Well-known Norwegian painters like Kittelsen, Erik Werenskiold, Christian Krohg, Axel Revold, Alf Rolfsen, and Svolvær's own Gunner Berg have been inspired by the scenery and the life of the town. Today there is a special house, called Kunstnerhuset, where artists may stay, and the Nordnorsk kunstnersentrum puts on permanent and special exhibitions. In the town hall hangs Gunnar Berg's well-known painting *Trollfjordslaget*, or the Battle of Trollfjord – a battle that was fought at the end of the last century between the fishermen in their small boats and the powerful steamship owners over a huge shoal of fish in the Trollfjord, a narrow strip of water with an even narrower entrance north-east of Svolvær. Gunnar Berg only just managed to finish the enormous painting, with its seven panels, before his untimely death at the age of 30.

KJERRINGØY GAMLE HANDELSSTED

In 1879 an impecunious writer called Knut Pedersen, who later became famous as Knut Hamsun, landed at Kjerringøy to borrow money from the owner of the trading centre, the legendary Erasmus Benedictus Zahl. Zahl lent him the money, and although Zahl was never repaid, Hamsun immortalized him as the genial, swashbuckling merchant Mack of Sirilund, who appears in the novels *Benoni* and *Rosa*. Hamsun's Sirilund is an exact description of Kjerringøy, and it was here that the Norwegian television series based on *Benoni* and *Rosa* was filmed.

If Zahl himself lacked Mack's more colourful qualities, he was a powerful personality in his own right. He arrived at Kjerringøy empty-handed in 1855, worked his way up, and in 1859 married the widow of the previous owner Ellingsen. From this time on everything he touched prospered: the shop, the fishing trade with Bergen, the export of fish roe to the Baltic. He was employer, counsellor, and banker to the people who lived round about, and when he died in 1900 he was the richest man in Nordland county. Like many of the merchants who held sway over such trading posts up and down the coast, Zahl was something of a benevolent despot, and Hamsun's character cast them in a new light: he replaced the traditional image of the kindly father figure with a more realistic picture of a man whose power in a small

beth. The house provides a vivid picture of the life of a prosperous merchant in the far north, where every luxury had to be imported at great cost and took months to arrive, where thrift was a necessary virtue. Thus, the front of the house, facing the sea and the main arrival route, was painted white, the most expensive colour, to impress visitors; the back part, however, which could only be seen from the courtyard, remained an economical yellow. Inside, a succession of reception rooms, where lavish hospitality was dispensed, are hung with hand-printed wallpaper from Paris and furnished with considerable style and expense, but the plain benches and tables in the room where the labourers ate are perhaps a clearer indication of ordinary life at the time. But if the utensils were simple, food was plentiful; the dependents demanded, and got, an assurance that salmon [a poor man's dish] was to be served not more than twice a week.

Upstairs, the bedrooms reflect even more the niceties of contemporary social convention. Starting with the sparsely furnished outer chamber for the outdoor servant girls, we work our way inwards via the housekeeper's comfortable bedroom to the luxurious four-poster of the master and mistress of the house.

Of the buildings grouped around a courtyard in the traditional Norwegian way, one of the most important was the *stabbur*, or storehouse, where provisions, extra bedding and other household goods were kept. The stabbur at Kjerringøy has a wonderful collection of handwoven rugs, made for the fishermen who spent the long winters in the Lofoten Islands, far from home and family. Much love and care went into the weaving, and each rug has its own individual pattern.

community was almost unlimited, and who did not shrink from social and sexual exploitation. Hamsun says of Mack: "[He] had the power to do anything he wished, whether good or bad, to a person. His soul was both black and white. He resembled his brother ... in that he could do whatever he wished; but he surpassed him every now and again in doing what he ought not to have done."

In the general store that supplied all the needs of the local population, there was a post and telegraph office and a licence to sell spirits. [Zahl, who disapproved strongly of drunkenness, did not make use of his licence.] The many-storied warehouse by the jetty is proof of the successful trade that was carried on: here fresh and dried fish were stored and local produce like cod liver oil, fish roe, berries, and down for stuffing quilts were treated and sold.

The main house was built in 1803 by Christian Sverdrup, the father of Zahl's wife Anna Elisa-

TRONDENES CHURCH

"There is no fairer church north of Trondheim than the church at Throndenæs [sic], which is a magnificent stone building, and has been splendidly decorated since olden times." This description of Trondenes Church in the county of Troms comes from an anonymous document dated 1591. The church's reputation for beauty had spread throughout the country; the priest Peder Claussøn wrote in 1613 that it "is held to be the fairest stone church to be found in a country village in Norway". And during the 1690s the priest and poet Petter Dass, of Alstahaug in Nordland county, wrote that "in the whole of Nordland there is not one that can be compared with it".

Of the 89 churches in Troms county, only Trondenes Church dates back to the Middle Ages. It is also the northernmost stone church in the country. It was built in 1220–50 in the reign of King Haakon Haakonsson, but before it there was another wooden church on the same site, built by King Øystein Magnusson at the beginning of the twelfth century, and before that again a pagan temple. The area was converted to Christianity early on; both the missionary kings, Olav Tryggvason [968–1000] and Olav Haraldsson, or St. Olav [995–1030], are known to have visited this part of the country. The first Christian baptism in the north of Norway is said to have been performed in the pool of Laugen near the church of Trondenes.

Just as Hammerfest Church expresses all the signs of having been built in the Space Age, so Trondenes Church is a visible witness to its own time. Instead of an optimistic upward flight, the building stands sturdily four-square on its site, arching its back against spiritual or worldly enemies. The churchyard wall was fortified, and traces can still be seen of the two fortified towers that stood below the choir facing the sea. The style is a mixture of romanesque and gothic, showing that the church was built at about the same time as Nidaros Cathedral was being completed. Several of the sculptors' signature marks are the same in both churches, and it is not improbable that they were loaned from Nidaros to Trondenes for the occasion.

The church's reputation for beauty was probably founded mainly on the many magnificent triptychs it contained, about eight or ten of them. Today the only ones left are the three in the choir. The main altar is an especially interesting piece, where the Blessed Virgin is the central figure, surrounded by a number of women relatives [most of them mythical] and their descendants. The husbands of these women have been relegated to the background. The oldest object in the church is the soapstone christening font, and the pulpit, with its paintings of the four evangelists, is from the mid-eighteenth century and is supposed to have been painted by Gottfried Ezekiel.

HAMMERFEST CHURCH

The church it is an ancient house,
And stands though its towers fall

One can hardly help thinking of these lines from a hymn by the Danish priest and poet N. F. S. Grundtvig when considering Hammerfest Church. For the church is indeed an ancient house in the world's most northerly town – the first church was built there in 1620 – and the buildings housing this particular church have replaced one another at what under the circumstances might be called a dizzying speed. Five times between 1684 and 1945 a church has been raised on this spot, and all except one of them have succumbed to fire.

At the end of the Second World War Hammerfest was razed to the ground. The only building left standing, no one knows why, was the little chapel in the graveyard, which served as a church until the new one was completed in 1961.

The design of the new church of Hammerfest has attracted a good deal of attention. However, the claim that it was inspired by the local distinctively shaped racks for drying fish is quite unfounded. The architect, Hans Magnus, has said that he took the idea from a church in Finland.

The clean, severe lines of the church rise defiantly, almost triumphantly, into the air. The interior continues the theme of simplicity, lightness, and soaring lines, and was decorated entirely by the artist Jardar Lunde. His glowing stained glass window in the wall behind the altar has taken Christ and the cross as its subject, but a Christ freed from the cross, proclaiming the resurrection and the life, and victory over darkness and death. The cross has been transformed into a Y, the symbol of longing, expressing man as adorer, worshipper. The artist has explained his idea as "the meeting between God and man – reconciliation and joy".

In spite of its history, the church still has some of the objects from previous churches, including the altarpiece from 1623 that had stood in the first church of all, and is now in the wedding chapel, two chandeliers from about 1750, and some very old silver. In the chapel attached to the church is a tablet of considerable artistic significance that was donated in 1744 to the second of the church buildings, and one of the bells is from the previous church.

ROCK CARVINGS

One day in 1972 a dynamite expert was called in by two householders near Bossekop, in Alta, to remove a large rock that they felt was spoiling their gardens. The expert examined the rock carefully to see whether it was possible to dynamite it, and discovered some extraordinary figures carved on its surface. Shortly afterwards, two small boys found some rock carvings nearby while they were out playing, and a man went out one evening to smoke a pipe and suddenly noticed a reindeer carved on a rockface.

The large rock, now known as Storsteinen, was never dynamited. One discovery led to another, and an enormous field of about 3000 rock carvings was revealed at the end of the Alta fjord – the largest field in Northern Europe created by a hunting people. Rock carvings may be carved, hacked, ground, or scratched on the rock surface. They represent people, animals, or objects, and it is not known whether the artists intended them to be works of art, to tell a story, or to have a symbolic and magical significance.

The rock carvings in Scandinavia date from about 6000 to about 4000 BC, and there are two types. The figures of animals, like reindeer, roe deer, and elk, and men hunting and trapping, were made by Stone Age hunters; later came a different set of carvings made by an agricultural people, which date from the Bronze Age. The latter carvings show the world of the farmer, people, boats, domestic animals, and tools, and petroglyphs of a symbolic nature, which are harder to identify. Sometimes the two types of carvings are found in the same area, like the Bardal field, in the innermost part of the Trondheim fjord, which has some of the largest hunting scenes known, side by side with monumental figures representing agricultural scenes.

The Hjemmeluft field in Alta is the largest field of hunting scenes, and spans the longest time period. It is thought that the carvings were made in the rocks down by the shore first of all, and that as the shoreline receded and the rocks became covered in moss and heather, new carvings were made on the lower slopes. If this is true, the highest carvings are the oldest.

It seems natural to speculate whether the motifs of the carvings have any connection with the Sami who used to live in the area. Some of the figures have drums and masks, and it may be that they were meant to represent shamans with *runebommer*, the magic drum used by the Sami. But whether or not they had any magical significance, they can still give us valuable information about the practical details of the hunting and fishing techniques used by Stone Age man.

Rock carvings made by hunters are found all along the Norwegian coast. On the west coast there are several large fields, including a very interesting one in Vingen in Nordfjord. Rock carvings depicting hunting scenes have even been found in wooded areas in eastern Norway and Trøndelag. But the richest and most lively Stone Age finds have been made in northern

parts of Norway.

Agricultural rock carvings are most wide-spread in the county of Østfold, but individual finds have been discovered in other parts of the country. After Østfold, the richest and certainly the strangest agricultural finds are in Trøndelag, where they differ very clearly from the carvings of the hunters. Here the ship is the most common motif, and people are more often part of the picture, as crews on board ship, in crowds, with weapons in their hands, or with raised genital organs. Domestic animals and tools, the sun and other fertility symbols are also found. Usually the figures are small and simple.

There have been many attempts to decipher the rock carvings, like the rock paintings in Spain and France, which are their equivalents. Historians, historians of comparative religion, art historians, and ethnographers have their different theories, but no one can really know what went on in the minds of the artists who made them and the contemporary hunters and farmers who appreciated them. Each one of us can form his own interpretation, and let his imagination wander back to prehistoric times when the world was new.

LAPPLAND – LAND OF THE SAMI PEOPLE

The Sami are a modern people. The reindeer herder in his colourful costume still exists, but today the reindeer harnessed to a sled has been mostly replaced by a snow scooter, and the blue felt costume by a practical overall.

The first means of livelihood that the Sami are known to have practised was hunting and trapping, along with the domestication of reindeer. Then they began to diversify, and until a few generations ago there were mountain Sami and shore Sami, river Sami and reindeer Sami, who exploited the natural resources around them in their different ways. Today the Sami are to be found at all levels of Norwegian society, and only a very small minority earn their living by reindeer herding. The only common trait left is their origin; they are all descendants of a hunting nomadic people who lived off the land.

The Sami culture of Nordkalotten, as the area of Norway, Sweden, and Finland north of the Arctic Circle is known, has many common characteristics that cut across the frontiers and apply to their history, religion, language, clothing, and crafts. On the other hand, there are also local variations that again are not dependent on frontiers, and that involve, for example, differences in clothing and in traditional ways of doing things. Over the centuries the Sami have sought to maintain and develop their culture in the face of at times considerable opposition from the authorities, who in certain periods have exerted very strong pressure on them to become Norwegianized. This resulted in many rejecting their own language and culture. In recent years, however, there has been a gradual change of policy, and now the Sami language is being used, Sami place names are being resumed, and Sami dress is being worn with pride. And fortunately the yoik, which is a Sami form of yodelling, for

generations forbidden at school, abused and considered an instrument of the devil, has survived, and the tradition is still carried on.

The Sami religion was a form of animism, in other words they believed that natural objects and phenomena are inhabited by spirits. The spirits of the ancestors were regarded as especially powerful, and were thought to abide in certain mountains, which they worshipped in the same way as they worshipped heavenly bodies and natural forces. Certain places, such as strangely shaped stones, were also regarded as the abode of spirits, and sacrifices were made there to ensure good luck in hunting and fishing. Bear and seal were regarded as sacred animals.

The *noaiden*, or shaman, functioned as an intermediary between humans and the spirit world, and made contact with the spirits by going into an ecstatic frenzy. For this he used his drum, or *runebomme*, which had a drumskin decorated with symbols. The shaman sang and danced while he drummed, until he fell into a coma, and his spirit left his body and went over to the other side to obtain advice and help. As shamanism began to lose ground the drum began to be used for making predictions instead, and probably this reinforced the old legends that attributed magic powers to the Sami.

The Sami have been very good at exploiting the resources of the north, fishing in the sea, lakes, and rivers, cultivating the land where it was arable and herding reindeer where it was not. Often it was necessary to combine these activities, since one alone did not provide enough to live on. Administrative decrees and frontier regulations between the Nordic countries have interfered with the Sami way of life, but a considerable number of them still continue with their time-honoured activities in this region of the north.

Karasjok – *Kárásjohka* – is Norway's next largest municipality in geographical extent, and 80 per cent of its population is Sami-speaking. Sami culture is still very much alive here, and a large number of Sami cultural monuments have been found in the region. Many of the most im-

portant Sami institutions are situated·here, and Karasjok functions in many ways as a Sami capital. It is even the seat of the Sami Parliament, a body of 39 representatives, who were elected for the first time in 1989 and deal with Sami affairs. The Sami Collections, *Samiid Vuorka-Davvirat*, are also housed in Karasjok, in a building designed by architect Vidar Corn. Jessen. The Col- lections, which were opened in 1972, present Sami history and culture throughout the Sami area, which includes other parts of central and southern Norway as well as the north. Sami history, industries, and handicrafts are exhibited, and there is also an open-air museum.

THE NORTHERN LIGHTS AND THE MIDNIGHT SUN

The Aurora Borealis, that firework display in the Arctic winter night, with its rapid sheets of darting, flickering light in vivid shades of yellow, green, red, and violet, has always been a source of mingled enchantment and terror, a symbol of who knows what natural forces at play in the heavens. The phenomenon is rare at lower latitudes, and there it has usually been interpreted as an omen of war or unrest or of a great fire. Up in the north people's attitude has been more relaxed; the northern lights appear rather too often to be a warning of war every time.

But the peoples of the north had their own superstitions in connection with the lights. The whole of Norway knows that it is dangerous to whistle at the northern lights, although the consequences of this frightful action vary locally. This belief probably derives from the general Nordic belief that the northern lights were the abode of the dead, and that contact could be made with them by whistling.

The northern lights have always made a deep impression on people, and acted as an inspiration to artists. The first mention in a Norwegian written source is found in the *The Elder Edda,* and they have proved a spur to the imagination of Norwegian writers ever since. Hamsun described them as a heavenly wedding feast. Jonas Lie chose to see them as a decorative welcome for those about to enter the kingdom of the dead. Many writers associate them with dancing or flights of ideas. Fridtjof Nansen wrote some of the most beautiful prose descriptions of the northern lights to be found in Norwegian literature in two of his books, complete with exquisite illustrations.

What causes the northern lights? They are the result of positively and negatively charged particles from the sun, which are caught in the earth's magnetic field and drawn into its atmosphere, where they collide with neutral gas particles. The gas is ionized and becomes charged with energy, which is emitted in the form of light. The phenomenon is particularly common in the areas around the earth's magnetic poles, and in the southern hemisphere it is known as the southern lights, or Aurora Australis.

The midnight sun is much simpler to understand; its movements are regulated, as we all know, by the movement of the earth around the sun. Its fame lies not so much in any mystery connected with it, as in the idea, extraordinary to most of the world, which lives between the Arctic and the Antarctic Circles, that the sun should shine at night. Like the northern lights, it has the spectacular beauty of a sunset, and usually forms the backdrop of some magnificent northern landscape or seascape. It also alters the rhythm of people's lives; the inhabitants of northern Norway tend to sleep little during the summer; they call on their friends in the middle of

the night and garden at two in the morning.

The Nordic countries naturally occupy a central position in research on the northern lights, and an observatory for this purpose was set up in Tromsø as early as 1928. In 1971 it was connected with the University of Tromsø, and now carries out studies of the northern lights, earth magnetism, and the ionosphere, among other things.

In 1989 the new Northern Lights Planetarium, designed by John Kristoffersen, was completed. The world's northernmost planetarium will guarantee experiences and journeys into the unknown that will not be easily forgotten, and can demonstrate both northern lights and the midnight sun all the year round.

Dates when the sun is entirely above the horizon:

Alta 18/5–27/6
Andenes 22/5–18/7
Bodø 4/6–8/7
Hammerfest 16/5–27/7
Harstad 25/5–18/7
Narvik 10/6–8/7
North Cape 13/5–29/7
Svolvær 28/5–14/7
Tromsø 20/5–20/7

The dates may change from year to year.

THE NORTH CAPE

Here I stand at the North Cape, at Finnmark's outermost point ... at the very end of the world... My curiosity is satisfied, and I shall return ... if God wills, to my homeland.

Thus spoke the first tourist to visit this outpost of the world, in 1664, the Italian priest and traveller Francesco Negri. The splendid isolation, and the idea of travelling to the end of the inhabited world, have attracted the adventurous ever since. Tempted by the thought of the midnight sun, they stay to marvel at the magnificence of the scenery, the vast panorama of sea and sky stretching unbroken to the Arctic Ocean and ultimately the North Pole.

The coast of Finnmark, warmed by the Gulf Stream, has been inhabited for 10,000 years. The original Sami inhabitants and the later Norwegian settlers made their living by fishing and reindeer herding. For thousands of years the cape was a local landmark, mostly for Norwegian and Russian sailors, but it was not until 1553 that it received its present name and became more widely known. In this year an Eng-

lish expedition under Sir Hugh Willoughby was sailing north along the Norwegian coast in search of a north-east passage to India and the Spice Islands, when a storm blew up off the Lofoten Islands and separated the ships. The *Edward Bonaventure* under Captain Richard Chancellor continued the journey northwards and finally reached the White Sea. He found no north-east passage, but instead a steep headland rising sheer from the sea, which he christened "the North Cape".

A tenuous English connection with the North Cape has persisted ever since. First they named it, then in the 1870s they made it the destination of a Cook's Tour, the first of many boatloads of tourists. In 1956 the first road to the North Cape was opened by Baron Fraser of North Cape, who had received the title for his part in the sinking of the German battle cruiser *Scharnhorst* off the Norwegian coast in 1943. The road made the Cape much more easily accessible; before this tourists came by boat and had to climb the 307

metres up to the plateau, often in stormy weather.

In 1929 the plateau was listed as a nature reserve. Since this is the most northerly latitude of growth for many plants, including heather, all animal and plant life was protected, and all further building was prohibited. As a result, chambers were hollowed out of the rock itself, and now the imposing North Cape Hall descends four storeys down into the cliff. Here can be found the Compass Café, in which the windows and seating arrangements follow the points of the compass, a souvenir shop, telecommunications centre and Europe's most northerly post office. In another chamber a huge screen of 225° shows views of the Cape at all seasons of the year. From here a tunnel lined with dioramas showing scenes from North Cape history leads through the mountainside to Europe's northernmost bar. A great glass window opens onto the sea and sky, protecting the visitor from the savagery of the elements while allowing him the illusion of being part of them.

Above ground, on the plateau, stands a pillar commemorating the visit of King Oscar II of Norway and Sweden in 1873. Another royal visitor was Louis Égalité, France's "citizen king", who visited the North Cape i 1795, during his exile.

NDEX

PHOTOGRAPHERS

Cover:
Heddal stavkirke: J.B. Olsen,
   R. Sørensen/NN/Samfoto
Kjeåsen, Hardanger: Pål Her-
   mansen/NN/Samfoto
Bryggen, Bergen: Mittet Foto
Nordlys: Mittet Foto
Nigardsbreen:Pål Hermansen/
   NN/Samfoto
Rødt og Hvidt (Edvard
   Munch): O. Væring

Birger Areklett/Samfoto: p. 42
Jan Arve Dale/Samfoto:
   p. 89
Dølabilde/Bård Bårdløkken:
   p. 12
Knut Evensen: pp. 44, 109
Terje Formoe: pp. 46, 47
Ragnar Frislid/NN/Samfoto:
   p. 113
Kim Hart/Samfoto: p. 29
Steinar Haugberg/Samfoto:
   p. 106
Pål Hermansen/NN/Samfoto:
   pp. 6, 83
Husmo Foto: pp. 11, 32, 36,
   55, 59, 71, 72, 77, 80, 85,
   86, 87, 93, 103
Industriarbeidermuseet,
   Vemork: p. 52
Lasse Jacobsen: p. 53
Knudsens Fotosenter: pp. 38,
   75, 79, 115
O.T. Ljøstad/Norsk Skogbruks-
   museum: p. 15
Nicolay Midthun: p. 65, at the
   bottom
Mittet Foto: pp. 18, 19, 23, 28
   (the small picture), 33, 34,
   37, 39, 41, 48, 56, 57, 60,
   62, 63, 64, 65, 67, 68, 69,
   107
Kjell Moltzau: pp. 96, 108
Lars Monsen/Trond Strømdahl:
   p. 111
Norsk Bergverksmusem:
   p. 51
NTB: p. 74 (the small picture)
Jørn Bøhmer Olsen/NN:
   pp. 21, 24, 91

Jørn Bøhmer Olsen/Rolf
   Sørensen/NN/Samfoto:
   pp. 4, 90 (the small pic-
   ture), 112
Per-Ludvig Pedersen: pp. 98,
   99
Polarsirkelsenteret: p. 101
Scanfoto: p. 27
Trygve Skramstad/Fædrelands-
   venden: p. 45
Leif Stavdahl/Maihaugen: p. 16
T. Suul/Nordenfjeldske Kunst-
   industrimuseum: p. 97
Helge Torsen: pp. 9, 73
O. Væring: p. 31
Helge Sunde/Samfoto: pp. 82,
   104
Jon Arne Sæter/Samfoto: p. 95

Highlights of Norway
© Gro Stangeland/
Boksenteret A/S, 1992
Based on an idea by: Gro
Stangeland
Cover design and layout:
Mette Lund Damsleth
Reproduction: Offset-Kopio
Printed by: New Interlitho, 1992
Produced by Boksenteret A/S

ISBN 82-7319-092-7

This book is one of the series of
quality books included in the
Cultural Programme of the
XVII Olympic Winther Games at
Lillehammer in 1994. It has been
published in collaboration with De
norske Bokklubbene A/S.

Lillehammer'94